UNCHARTED

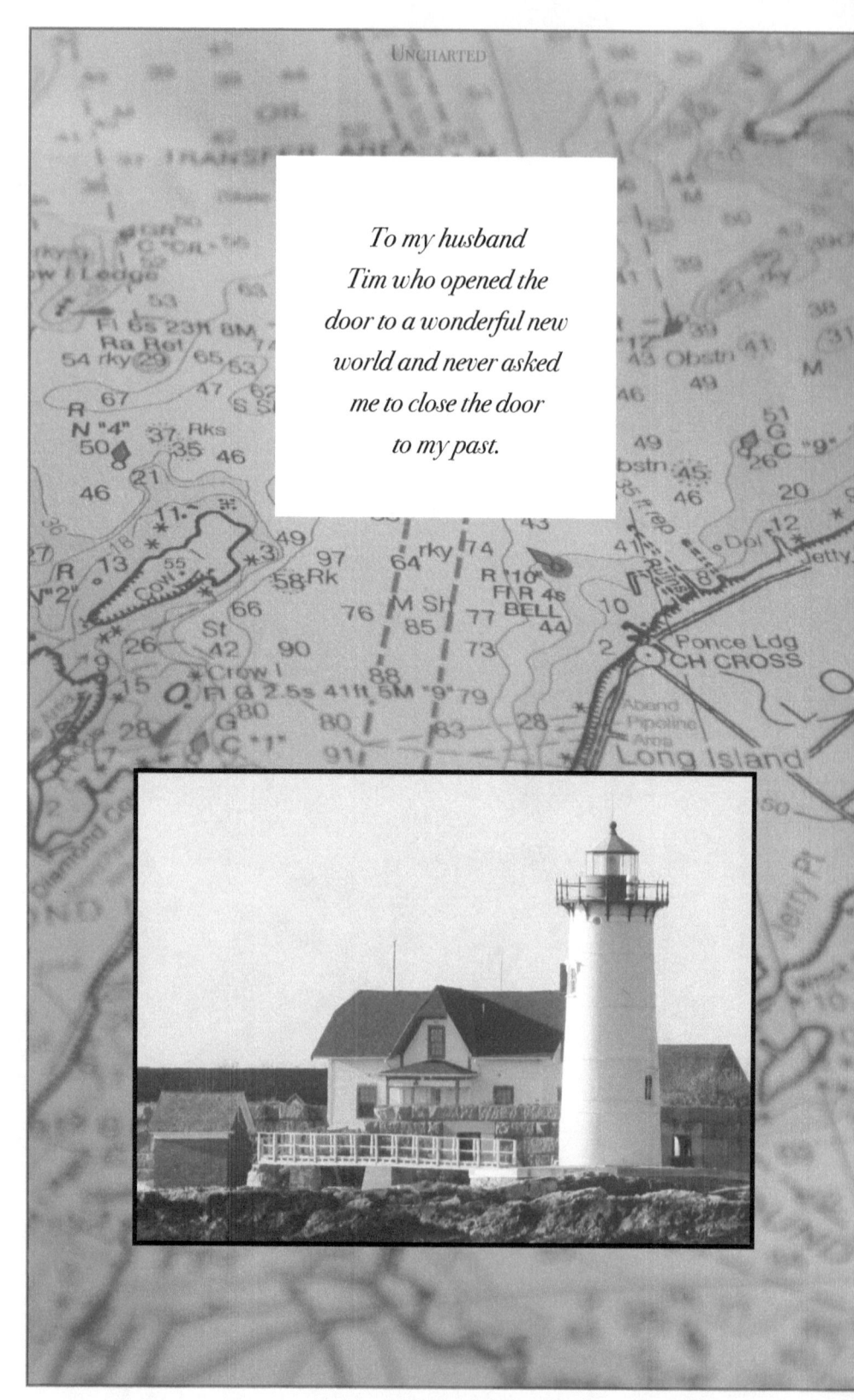

*To my husband
Tim who opened the
door to a wonderful new
world and never asked
me to close the door
to my past.*

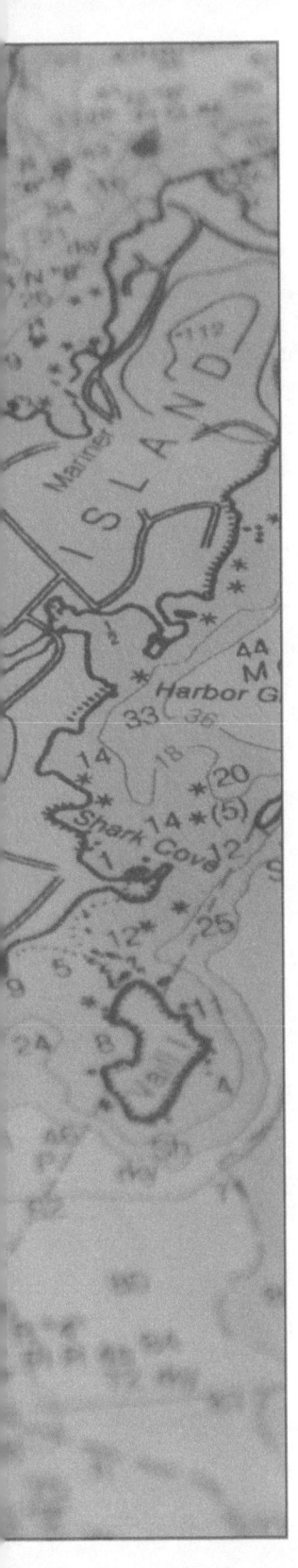

BARBARA A. BUSENBARK

UNCHARTED

*A widow's journey back to life and love
cruising the Intracoastal Waterway*

ISBN: 979-8-9894725-0-5 (Paperback)
ISBN: 979-8-9894725-1-2 (Hardcover)
ISBN: 979-8-9894725-2-9 (EPUB)

Library of Congress Catalog Number: 2023923780

Color Notes Publishing
4462 Pro Am Ave. E.
Bradenton, FL. 34203
www.colornotespublishing.com
Barbara@BarbaraBusenbark.com

Produced by Peter E. Randall Publisher
5 Greenleaf Woods Drive, U102
Portsmouth, NH 03801

Printed in the United States of America

Cover art and design by Barbara A. Busenbark

Contents

CHAPTER I

BROKEN

The world breaks everyone, and afterward,
some are strong at the broken places.
But those that will not break it kills.
—Ernest Hemingway

I am a landscape painter, or at least I was at the time. For five years my husband, Rick, and I ferried my paintings to summer art festivals from Maine to Pennsylvania. Each year my inventory of art show supplies grew until my SUV could no longer accommodate the paintings, display panels, and tent.

Two weeks before Christmas in 2011, Rick bought me a used van. He planned to revamp it for the following summer's art shows, but next summer never came.

On that chilly December morning, he drove the van home, pulled it into the garage, and started taking out the bench seats.

"Do you know what you're going to do?" I asked.

He tapped his temple. "I've got it all up here."

He spent all afternoon in the garage.

That evening after dinner, we settled down to watch TV. Rick complained about his acid reflux. Before the end of the program, he retired upstairs in search of relief. When the eleven o'clock news finished, I checked in on him.

Rick sat in his recliner, still uncomfortable.

"Would you get me some Tums?" he asked.

"Sure."

I returned with the tablets and put them in his outstretched hand.

"You don't have to wait up with me," he said.

"It's fine, I'm up. I'll wait with you until the medicine works."

"I love you," he said. Those were the last words he ever spoke, leaving me forever.

After a sudden release of air, he lost consciousness. I ran to the phone and called 9-1-1. A police officer drove me to the hospital while the EMTs attended to Rick. I stared out the window of the police car into the dark night and prayed, Oh, dear God, please don't take him, please.

We reached the hospital, and the officer walked me to the emergency room and unfolded a metal chair leaning against the wall. The chair was cold, the room was cold, everything was cold. Gravity hung in the air with the weight of silence. The antiseptic hospital smell reinforced the fear that death was inescapable. Without windows, the bright lights and white walls made the room impervious to the darkness outside. The doctor stood by a stainless steel table in the center of the room, waiting for Rick. I kept repeating, No, no, this can't be.

An EMT performing chest compressions straddled Rick's body as they wheeled him in on a gurney. When the EMT climbed down, the doctor put his stethoscope on his ears and Rick's chest. As though in slow motion, the doctor removed the stethoscope, looked up at me, and shook his head.

Rick was gone.

"No, you don't understand. He's the love of my life," I said, as though that would make any difference.

"I'm very sorry," the doctor said.

Everyone left the room.

"Oh, Rick," I whispered, as though he'd forgotten his keys or left a door open or missed an item on the grocery list. What else could I say? There were no unspoken words between us. He was gone. Thirty-two years and still not enough time with him. I closed his eyes the rest of the way and left the room, too sad to cry, too lost to understand what had happened.

A receptionist showed me to a waiting room. "Is there someone I can call for you?"

Everything had blurred into a haze of sorrow.

She called our son, Richard, living in Nashua, an hour away, while I curled up in the fetal position on the waiting room couch. Richard arrived at some point. I had lost track of time.

"Where is he?" Richard asked with tears in his eyes.

"Down the hall, first door." I pointed the way.

Richard went to say goodbye to his father.

Later, Richard drove me home, where I cried myself to sleep. I stayed on my side of the bed, hoping I'd wake up and Rick would be on his side. He wasn't and never would be again. I would continue to cry myself to sleep, night after night.

Richard stayed to help. While I slept, he called friends and family to let them know about Rick. He had spent four years in the navy. With his big personality, Richard always dominated the room. I could depend on his help.

When I woke, I went downstairs and walked into the kitchen. Richard and Jim (one of my brothers) sat at the counter drinking coffee.

They didn't know what to do with me. I didn't know what to do with me.

Then the phone rang.

It was Kathy, my neighbor, offering her condolences. I thanked her for the kind gesture and phoned Mark, Rick's best friend. I don't remember what I said. Disbelief and sorrow merged to form a fog of amnesia. While I went through the motions of functioning I began to doubt whether the past I remembered ever existed. My anchor, my world no longer held me in place, and I drifted through time. I could barely speak. I couldn't eat. Nothing would ever be the same. I would never be the same.

In the afternoon, family and friends gathered in the living room. Conversations drifted around me. I sat on the couch, comforted but silent. The familiarity of family chatting filled the void, but Rick's absence made the scene disorienting. He should have been there. I didn't understand my life without him. That would take time.

❋ ❋ ❋

On Monday, we met with the funeral director. I'd driven by the large white house with black shutters on Pine Street hundreds of times. Now it became a destination to confront, with a door I didn't want to walk through. My family came with me. The office door faced the driveway. A row of windows, dressed with sheer curtains, lit the off white walls of the nondescript room. Are funeral homes designed to be bland, colorless, and lifeless?

I sat on the couch, my brother Joe sat in the chair by the desk, and an assistant brought another chair for Jim. The questions for Rick's obituary began. Where was he born, date of birth, parents, siblings, schooling, job title.

"Reliability engineer," I replied.

"Where did he get his degree in engineering?"

I explained the coursework and Six Sigma certifications Rick had earned from the University of Arizona, but this foolish man didn't understand. Rick had gone to night school to become a technician and over the last twenty years worked his way up to senior reliability engineer, but his degree was in music composition. The funeral director wouldn't put engineer in Rick's obituary. I was broken, with no fight in me, and I let it go.

"Father Belanger is out of town, so the funeral will be Thursday."

"Isn't there another priest?" Joe asked.

His forehead scrunched up in confusion when the funeral director responded in the negative. Joe didn't understand life in a small town. He lived and worked in New York City, where multiples of everything abound. Joe struggled to be patient. We were on New Hampshire time. There was no "New York minute."

At home, I gathered clothes for Rick—his suit, white shirt, and blue tie with the Peanuts characters playing musical instruments. Then I picked up the oversized, gold colored key I had bought at an antique shop in Denver three months earlier. Rick knew what it was when I gave it to him. I handed the clothes and key to Jim for the funeral home.

Jim looked puzzled.

"This needs to go with him." I tried to hold back tears. "When we were first married, we visited an antique shop. Once we were outside, Rick told me to close my eyes and put out my hand." I took a deep breath. "I opened my eyes and saw a skeleton key in my hand." The tears flowed. "Rick told me it was the key to his heart. I found this one in an antique store in Denver and thought I'd give him a bigger damn key." Laughing and crying, I told Jim, "This has to go with him, and I want a closed casket. I can't see him like that."

"I'll tell them. It's whatever you want," Jim said.

I knew I could count on him to deal with things I could not.

Rick was romantic. The key to his heart marked the beginning of thirty years of gestures that assured me his love was forever. He wrote me love poems. Each anniversary he gave me a gift according to the year: first anniversary, paper; second anniversary, cotton; third anniversary, leather, and so on. For thirty-two years. For my fiftieth birthday, he wrote a song for me. No other gift before or since has seized my heart with such intensity. It brought tears to my eyes. A song I will never hear again.

I retreated to the kitchen; I had family to feed. In times of stress, cooking, particularly making a pot of spaghetti sauce, brought comfort. I didn't even know what I'd make with the sauce, but at least I had something to do.

As I stirred the pot, the phone rang.

"I'm so sorry about Rick." It was Aunt Kathleen from Louisville. I knew she understood. Her husband, Uncle Dick, had died years ago.

"Thanks, Aunt Kathleen."

"You know I'd be there if I could."

"No, no, I understand."

Age had become a factor. Aunt Mary called, saying the same thing. Travel was too much for them. Hearing their voices provided comfort enough.

"What are you doing?" she asked.

"Making spaghetti sauce."

"What? You should be drinking!"

That made me smile. It would be some time before I laughed again.

The part of me that talked too much and laughed easily died with Rick. The depth of pain and sorrow overwhelmed me, sucked up my self-confidence, and spit out a fragile, indecisive woman. Being alive was a burden. I didn't want to live without Rick. His death extinguished a spark within me. I wondered how the sun continued to rise and set. He believed in me in a way no one else ever would. He completed me. Without Rick, I was no longer whole.

CHAPTER 2

ALONE

*When something bad happens you
have three choices. You can either let it define you,
let it destroy you, or you can let it strengthen you.*
—Theodor Seuss Geisel

Three hours in public for Rick's wake, even with family for support, seemed impossible. I feared I couldn't control the sorrow consuming me. I needed to keep my hell private. In my world, there could be no public outburst. The fragrance of flowers saturated the air in the funeral parlor. I stood by the closed coffin, sons Richard and Mike alongside me. I placed Rick's favorite guitar on a stand nearby, along with pictures of him.

My dread melted away when I felt all the love. People assembled at the funeral home filed by with hugs and wonderful memories. It lifted my spirits. I comforted men in tears. Together, we all loved Rick.

For months, family and friends held me together with love and compassion. Each time I sensed a piece of myself sinking beneath the waves of sorrow, they pulled me back.

"She's tough, she'll be fine," my brother Joe told my sister-in-law

Debbie when she expressed concerns about me. That simple sentence gave me faith in myself when I had none.

In January, my brother Bob and his wife, Barbara, came to visit. Winter slowed the work requirements for them. I welcomed their company.

The mind plays terrible tricks on a broken heart. It caught me off guard when Barbara picked up a torn piece of purple surgical glove lying on the ground in front of my house.

"What's this?" she asked.

"It's from that night."

For weeks it lay frozen on the ground, left behind by an EMT. I couldn't bring myself to touch it. That would only confirm the reality I didn't want to accept, a tangible reminder of that night. Somehow, she understood, and I never saw it again. Relieved of the burden of looking at it and doing something with it, I edged closer to peace. The tension I had created around a piece of latex faded away like a whisper in the wind.

At the end of the week, Bob and Barbara flew back home to Seattle, leaving me alone, almost. Tigger, my rescued dog—small, blond, and shaggy—evoked smiles and comfort. Days when I desperately missed Rick and wanted to stay in bed and cry, I got up for Tigger. The morning routine of feeding him and walking outside, acknowledged by his wagging tail, brought continuity to my shattered world.

It was Tigger's turn to rescue me.

Less than a decade before, I had longed to be left alone. The barrage of kids, work, and the school board dominated my life. It didn't matter what door I walked through, there were questions and requests that needed a response.

Home: "Mom, what's for dinner?" "Is my baseball uniform clean?" "Do we have any poster board for my science project?" "Barb, can you get the car inspected? I can't get time off."

Work: "Can you put aside what you're doing and help Dave design a logo for the project he's working on?"

School board: "Does the technology committee have a figure for the budget, or do you want to do another warrant article? We need a number by the end of the month."

By contrast, I enjoyed barn chores. They restored my calm and distracted me from everyday pressures. Imagine looking forward to shoveling shit. Nobody else wanted to join in that activity. Smokey, my horse, would try to get her muzzle in my jacket pocket looking for treats, and follow me around the pasture as I pushed my wheelbarrow. The simplicity of it delighted me.

This once noisy home was now mute, with no laughter, music, or quarreling brothers. I wandered from room to room like a ghost, barely there, Tigger following close behind. Every door transformed into a portal to the past. I looked for answers.

What do I do with the rest of my life?

The living room, long and narrow, stretched out in front of me. With the help of a crowbar, paint, and hard work, we had transformed the dark, muddled cave of paneling and dank smelling orange shag carpeting into the heart of family time. Saturday nights, I'd sit on the couch with my boys, the scent of popcorn wafting from the kitchen as the kids yelled to Rick, "Hurry, the show's gonna start."

The sunroom cheered me, my favorite room in the house. Sunlight poured in on the slate flooring we had installed one New Year's Eve, forgoing the annual party. It absorbed the heat and warmed the house. The large sliding doors looked out on the yard and the woods beyond. Occasionally, a bear came by if I forgot to bring in the bird feeders at night.

Between the living room and kitchen, a cozy room with a wood stove and rocking chair provided respite. I loved spending the morning stoking the crackling fire after a weekend snowstorm. A thick blanket of snow brought a stillness to the earth.

I wondered if that peaceful feeling would ever return.

Newly fallen snow no longer brought thoughts of calm and

tranquility. Now dread lingered. The Mathewson Company plowed the driveway. After every storm Rick would clear paths to the propane tanks and my studio, coercing our geriatric snowblower into service with unlimited patience and a bucket of tools. Even if I could start it, maneuvering the rusty, red beast through snowbanks exceeded my abilities. There were no snowstorms that winter. I thought about all the prayers offered on my behalf and wondered if divine intervention was a factor in the weather.

Mike's bedroom, with its border tape of Labrador retrievers, reminded me of the little boy who loved animals and books about dinosaurs. He had moved to Miami and now lived with friends, no longer a little boy. I knew I needed to strip the wallpaper and border tape filled with black, chocolate, and white Labs, but it didn't erase the fond memories.

I stepped into Rick's office. It used to be Richard's bedroom before he joined the navy. Now he had a house of his own. Rick replaced posters of cool cars and snowboarding with the Picasso print of Three Musicians I had bought him. I opened the closet door and stared at the five guitar cases lined up. Music had filled the house when friends came over to jam, during band rehearsal, or when Rick practiced. The stillness of his guitar strings created a heartbreaking silence. Rick's music was his voice.

As I turned to continue down the hall, a smile ached to cross my face. During Richard's term in the navy, Mike had lured me into believing he had matured. He met the request to clean his room quickly and efficiently. I should have known better. When Richard announced he was coming home on leave, I opened his bedroom door to put fresh sheets on the bed. A disaster of Mike's making stood before me. For months, instead of cleaning his room, Mike had thrown all his mess into Richard's room and closed the door. It was an occasion to whip out his middle name, and he knew what that meant.

As a little boy, Mike had once asked, "How come you call me Michael John when you're mad at me instead of Mikey?" At thirteen, he needed no explanation.

Room after room, memory after memory, two realities set in. Without Rick's income, I wouldn't be able to afford the mortgage payments. Maintenance of the house and four acres of land required many hands. With a full house, we all had chores—mowing the lawn, shoveling snow, doing laundry, cleaning the chimney, stacking wood, weeding the gardens. Taking care of the animals; a horse, two pygmy goats, two dogs, and a cat also required attention. Now, only one dog, Tigger, remained, but the other chores still needed attention.

It all fell on my shoulders. I listed the house for sale.

After six months I decided to deal with Rick's music equipment. Besides his guitars, recording equipment, and harmonicas, a plethora of miscellaneous devices filled plastic bins. Mark and Cheryl, who were bandmates with Rick and friends of ours, came over to help sort through it all. I didn't know what a lot of the items were or their value.

Cheryl took pictures of each item while Mark logged them on a spreadsheet. During the process, Mark reached into a bin, pulled out a device with a small screen and some buttons, and said, "Hey, this is mine."

We all laughed.

"What is it?" I asked.

"It's a decibel meter. Most musicians are deaf because they never used one."

The next week, Mark researched the value of everything and volunteered to help sell the equipment. It was important to sell the guitars to people I knew. It felt as if the instruments were pieces of Rick. Some items I donated to South Meadow School for its music department. As the principal helped me unload Rick's music stand from the car, I began to tear up.

"I thought I'd be better by now."

"It's going to take a very long time."

CHAPTER 3

HOME

When you're safe at home you wish you were having an adventure;
when you're having an adventure you wish you were safe at home.
—Thornton Wilder

I knew little of grief, only sadness, as when my parents had died. Grief is different. Time does not heal the wound. Time grants the experience to learn how to continue to live. The quiet that engulfed me in my solitude fluctuated between reconciling the life I thought I'd be living and the uncertain future waiting for me.

Everyone's future is uncertain. Many things happened in my life that sent me in different directions. For years, a house full of kids, animals, a husband, and a job created a sense of treading water to stay afloat. I had a good idea of what to expect each day, but I had no time to pursue my creative interests. In time the kids grew up, and then my mother became ill. I quit my job as a creative director to take care of her.

In between visits from my home in New Hampshire to New Jersey to see her, time opened up for me. I hadn't painted in years, and I'd missed it.

"I thought you weren't interested in painting anymore," Rick had said.

Those words, seemingly benign, stung. As a musician, Rick once understood the creative urges I needed to follow, whether writing or painting. In college, we had imagined a life together where he'd write the music, and I'd write the words. Then we grew up and got proper jobs, but the desire to create never faded.

He saw the astonishment on my face turn into sadness. At that moment, Rick made it his mission to help me return to painting. After a shopping trip to Boston, I had a proper easel, fresh oil and water-color paints, brushes, canvases, sketch pads, and paper. Everything I needed. The cost stunned me when the cashier tallied the order.

"It's the cost of one of my guitars. Don't worry about it," Rick said as he loaded everything into the SUV. He believed in me more than I believed in myself.

The frustrations that go with a painter's life threatened to derail me, but Rick would have none of it.

"I suck," I'd whine.

"No! You create paintings from nothing. You don't suck. I have a degree in music, but I just play other people's songs. You're good. You've made more money selling paintings than I ever made playing music."

With Rick's encouragement, my painting career progressed to where we planned to move to the seacoast, where I could open a gallery. When Rick retired, he would run the business. As a first step, we readied the house to sell and listed it in the spring. In the winter the real estate market slowed, so we removed the listing. When Rick died, the dream of having a gallery faded. I didn't know if I could establish a business alone. Still, I listed the house again not knowing where I'd go when it sold.

The solace of staying in town fed my trepidation about starting a new life on the seacoast. There was much to love about living in Peterborough. For thirty years, I called it home, longer than I'd lived anywhere else. We renovated three houses, raised our kids there, coached baseball, volunteered in the schools, and made many friends. Running errands invariably led to seeing friends and acquaintances and stopping to chat.

Memories begged me to stay, but reminders threatened to drown me in sadness. After Rick died, there were condolences for months, everywhere I went. The men at the recycling center helped me with my trash. At the filling station, Ken, the school district's technology coordinator, pulled up to the pumps behind me and asked to embrace me. At the town hall, the town clerk came out from behind the counter for a hug.

On display in the town hall is a painting I made of the fire department's antique truck. I donated the commissioned painting as a fundraiser and presented it to the town at the Fireman's Ball. My life was interwoven with the town. Starting a new life surrounded by my past wasn't possible. Everywhere I went, reminders of my past life brought back memories.

History blended with daily life in Peterborough. Historic buildings with hardwood floors lined Grove Street. At times I allowed my imagination to drift back to the days of the horse and buggy. As I strolled downtown, I would conjure up scenes of women in long dresses with the sound of clip-clopping horses in the background.

When we first moved to town, a strange sight caught our attention. An older gentleman rode down Main Street on horseback with a goat following. In time we learned the man was Captain Milton Fontaine with his horse, Sarge. A companion animal for Sarge, the goat escaped one day and followed them into town. Seeing no harm done, the goat continued to accompany Mr. Fontaine and Sarge on their treks to the post office.

Our first house in Peterborough provided the opportunity to learn the meaning of "sweat equity." Built as a warehouse for the mill down the street, it had been converted into a home. We lived on a tight budget and heated the house with wood, unable to afford oil for the furnace. The year we moved in I learned how to use a maul to split logs Rick had cut to stove length with his chainsaw. After five years of spending every spare moment making improvements, we sold our little house on Wilder Road, made a good profit, and moved into a larger house.

We could now afford oil for the furnace. I called the local oil company to set up delivery and found out what living in a small town meant. I identified myself, never having dealt with the company before, and the woman on the other end said, "Oh, yeah, across the street from the Browns." How she knew who I was and where I lived took ten more years of living in Peterborough to find out.

Situated a short walk to town, our second Peterborough home stood for one hundred years. A merchant had owned the house in the 1800s and worked in one of the shops downtown. The house's solid oak newel post, just inside the front door, had a ball top the size of a softball. Worn smooth by the many hands it had known, the unpainted post and handrail guided generations of families up the stairs. In living there, we became part of the house's history.

Mount Monadnock completed the environs, rising in the distance, visible from every high point in town. The natural beauty of the area provided a serene backdrop to our lives, a buffer to the troubled world beyond. The brilliant foliage in autumn turned a drive down the road magical, with glowing yellows and fluorescent oranges arching overhead.

I knew I needed to move forward, but I remained frozen, unable to make any consequential decisions. I worried the house would sell before I knew what to do. Panic struck the first time the realtor asked to show the house. Mary Anne, my sister-in-law, called. I told her I didn't know what to do if the house sold.

"You don't have to decide the rest of your life right now," she said.

That comment became my mantra.

The depressed real estate market led to few showings, so my fears of having to leave in a hurry dissipated. My feelings of uncertainty did not.

Maintenance issues plagued me. I kept making improvements, hoping the house would sell. At first, I looked at smaller houses in Peterborough. I ventured over to the seacoast to consider my options. House hunting and travel became the conduits to finding my way. Each trip, near or far, took me away from reminders of what I had lost and closer to knowing who I was.

In February, my cousin Mary from Louisville called and asked if I wanted to join her in Florida during Kentucky Derby week. She had planned an escape to avoid throwing a derby party. Friends expected Mary to host the annual event, but she didn't feel up to it. Instead, Mary and her friend Rosie rented a condo on the beach in Indian Rocks. I just needed to get myself down there.

I couldn't refuse the invitation. My friend Diane advised me to travel as much as I could, and this opportunity sounded delightful. The trip gave me something to look forward to when my future looked like a jungle with only a butter knife to clear my path.

Mary and I shared a special bond. We were like the sisters we never had. Growing up, we wrote letters back and forth, and as adults, our mothers kept us up to date on each other's activities. Distance never kept us apart. I valued Mary's counsel. I counted on her to help with life decisions, and I welcomed time away from the house.

"I'm working on a series of paintings," I told her as we sat on the beach in Florida. "Main streets across the country."

"That sounds fun," she replied.

"Maybe I should write a book to go along with the paintings. A little history about the places."

"No, no. That's way too much. You'll never finish either. Just work on the paintings."

The next day, my son Mike, who lived in Miami, made the three-hour drive to join Mary, Rosie, and me for a couple of days. After too much sun, we craved a break. Mike offered to drive. We traveled south on Gulf Boulevard, not sure where we would end up. A tall blue and white sign said, Psychic Readings. Totally out of character, I pointed to the little building next to the sign and blurted, "Mike, pull in there!"

"You're not serious, are you?" Mike asked.

"Yeah, just pull in."

I wanted to get a reading, to hear something about my future. Truth be damned.

Rosie wanted a reading too. Mary and Mike stayed in the car, shaking their heads in disbelief. Rosie entered first, then it was my turn. The psychic had a quizzical look on her face.

"There's a presence behind you, holding you back."

I stiffened, knowing Rick was that presence. Wary of being a fool and giving her specific information to feed back to me, I said nothing.

"You have a yellow aura. That says you're intelligent with a lot of positive energy. You're very creative. Why are you so worried? You're going to be fine."

I heard little beyond having a presence behind me and that I'd be fine.

Farther down the coast, we stopped at the funky, little town of Gulfport on Boca Ciega Bay. Cute shops and restaurants painted bright hues lined Beach Boulevard. The color combinations looked like scenes in cartoons or fairy tales, pinks and greens, blues and purples. Live oak trees dripping with Spanish moss gave an old-world vibe. A huge vintage Florida postcard mural brought life to an outside wall on the corner of Beach and Shore Boulevards. It was an enchanting place.

A carefree week of going to the beach, dining out, drinking, and dancing created space to relax. I confided in Mary about the gallery idea. She encouraged me to go for it and said she'd help me decorate. Her bright smile and warmth inspired me. Anything was possible with Mary. Her faith in me raised my confidence. I returned to Peterborough with a more positive outlook about my future, uncertainty notwithstanding.

Spring arrived, bringing with it outside chores. I needed to learn how the riding mower worked. I'd never been on the damn thing. That was Mike and Rick's job.

I entered the garage and confronted John Deere. The key was in the ignition. A sticker explaining how to start it adhered to the space between the footrests. I studied the instructions. An acre of overgrown lawn needed mowing. Time to saddle up and ride.

John Deere and I became well acquainted, particularly when I got hung up on a tree stump. I was at a loss for how to free it. I called my son Richard, who lived an hour away.

"The tractor got stuck on a tree stump," I said.

"Got stuck? Or you got it stuck? Okay, you still have your truck, right?" he asked.

"Yeah."

"The chain Dad had in the garage in the oil pan, is that still there?"

"Yeah." I wasn't sure I liked where this was going. I wanted him to drop everything and come save me.

"Okay, put the John Deere in neutral, and attach the chain to it. Attach the other end to the truck, then give it a little tug."

It worked. I freed the tractor. It was a small thing, but I felt triumphant.

Regardless of my victory, my search for a new home continued. I couldn't keep up with the work the property required. I traveled to the seacoast to look at a few houses. One house, a humble ranch on Route One in Hampton Falls, lingered in my thoughts. It needed a lot of work, but the price and location made it appealing. I'd refurbished three houses in the past, but Rick and I had worked on them together. I struggled with making such a monumental decision.

CHAPTER 4

GOING PLACES

I've been absolutely terrified every
moment of my life—and I've never let it keep me
from doing a single thing I wanted to do.
—Georgia O'Keeffe

My brother Bob called and invited me to visit him and Barbara in Seattle.

"I could drive across the country," I said.

"No, you're not driving alone across the country."

I let his words sink in and came up with another plan. I could take the train from Boston to Seattle. It was a safe way to see the country and make an adventure out of the invitation. I continued to develop an itinerary that included a stop in Montana. Bob agreed that this was a much better plan.

One stitch at a time I tried to bind my broken heart with the threads of time and travel. Healing required patience, something I never had much of. The process put me on a path of self-discovery. By stepping away from my everyday life I was able to gain perspective, to see the world differently. I had to accept the changes before me, but I couldn't yet embrace the future. This trip took me one more step toward figuring out where I was going. A cross-country train trip gave me something to look forward to instead of this black hole of uncertainty.

A week before I was to board the train, Mary called. Her serious tone concerned me. She started with, "I wanted to let you know before I sent out an email to the whole family." I braced myself, remembering our conversations about some recurring symptoms she'd had for the last nine months. "I have pancreatic cancer."

Stunned, I tried to continue listening as she spoke about the next steps and options, but my heart crumbled. When I got off the phone, I looked up everything I could about the prognosis. None of it encouraged me.

Please God, not her too.

Mary's chemo treatments started the same day I left for Seattle. Mike had moved in with Richard and volunteered to take care of Tigger during my trip. Mike referred to it as a "walkabout," the solitary journey into the wilderness made by young Aboriginal men as a rite of passage. Though I was neither Aboriginal nor male, the concept still worked for me. I needed to learn what it meant to be alone.

Mike drove me to the Back Bay train station, and I thought of Mary. Our journeys carried us in opposite directions. Mary was facing death, and I was trying to put it behind me.

As I stood on the platform, track five, a digital clock suspended from the ceiling marked the time. I was early. The stagnant air had the musty smell of every train tunnel, and it was ten degrees cooler than up at street level. Daylight from the tunnel entrance splashed on the wall before the curve in the tracks.

The train station was located less than a mile away from where Rick and I had met thirty years earlier. A transit map divided the east and westbound tracks. Crisp white dots on the Green Line marked familiar stops along Huntington Avenue: Northeastern University, Symphony Hall, Prudential Center, and the Museum of Fine Art. Like stepping-stones into my past, the dots propelled me back in time, six weeks into my nineteenth year, the night I'd met Rick. It was 1978.

"Last call," bellowed the bartender at the Cask 'n Flagon.

Objections cut the air, thick with the stench of stale beer.

"It's still early," my friend said.

"Come party with us," a voice behind me called out.

I turned. A tall man with broad shoulders, a mustache, and dark, shoulder-length hair stood behind me.

"Sure," my friend answered. He was always up for a party.

We followed the stranger and his friends past the bouncers, out the swinging doors, and up the short flight of stairs to Huntington Avenue. We got acquainted as we walked through the alley to their apartment building on the Fenway.

Rick, the tall stranger, and I sat at the kitchen table and continued our conversation. After a quick beer, my friends emerged from the living room and announced it was time to go.

"I'll walk you home whenever you say," Rick said.

"Oh no, you're coming with us," my roommate, Joanne, demanded.

I looked at Rick. I trusted him, even though we'd met less than an hour before. After all, he was from Iowa.

"I'm all right," I answered.

My friend Marita, a beautiful brunette with dark brown eyes and a devilish smile, peered at me. "Are you sure?"

"Yes."

"Okay, everybody, we're outta here." Marita headed for the door, and with a wave, motioned for the rest to follow.

After a while, I asked Rick to walk me home. When we reached my dorm, he asked if he could kiss me. I said yes. Then he asked for my phone number and gave me his. At two in the morning, I opened the door to my dorm room, where Joanne was already asleep. The hall phone rang. Who would call at 2:00 a.m.?

"Hello?" I answered.

"Barb?"

"Yeah."

"I just wanted to see if you'd given me your real phone number. Good night," Rick said.

"Good night."

In the silent hall of the dorm, I strained to hear the click, signaling he'd ended the call. Still, my hand remained on the receiver as though it would keep us connected. A smile I couldn't suppress grabbed hold of me. Smitten, beguiled, charmed. My heart danced while my head tried to understand the frenzy of emotions I felt. My footsteps echoed through the empty hall as I returned to my room.

That night changed the trajectory of my life. I thought I knew my future. Growing up in New Jersey in the shadow of New York City, I loved the fast pace, swirl of activity, and energy of the city. Every trip to New York, whether visiting the Metropolitan Museum of Art to see the Arms and Armor exhibit or Madison Square Garden to watch the Rangers play hockey, convinced me that's where I wanted to live. If I worked hard, maybe someday I'd write for *The New York Times*.

When I imagined my future self, I saw a woman rushing through the city, hailing a cab or chasing a news story, and living in a small apartment near Central Park. That dream wasn't to be. A year after I met Rick, a seismic shift brought that vision crashing down. At twenty, I left college to marry Rick. The small wedding didn't match the plans my parents had had for their little girl. Seven months later, our son Richard was born.

Incarcerated by adulthood, my dreams and aspirations morphed into challenges and responsibilities. Richard's birth dictated the course of my adult life. I worked hard at motherhood to atone for my original sin of having a child before I was ready and the shame of being pregnant when I got married.

Shortly after Richard's second birthday, we bought a house in West Peterborough, New Hampshire, the only place we could afford. It needed work, but we were young and full of enthusiasm and energy. With only two houses nearby and woods all around, we began our country life. A woodstove sat in the middle of the living room and, for the first four years, provided our only source of heat.

Rick started working on a production line and returned to school at night. I waitressed until Rick advanced to technician and landed a job at Digital Equipment Corporation, a leader in technology. I took out student loans and finished my degree in English literature. A few months later, Mike's birth completed our family. Instead of the *New York Times*, I worked at the *Peterborough Transcript* and the *Monadnock Ledger* in Peterborough, New Hampshire, and eventually *BYTE* magazine. I had no regrets. It wasn't the life I'd dreamed of. It surpassed my dreams. Only the very lucky ever know that kind of love. When Rick died, our grand love story ended.

Passengers crowded onto the train platform and broke me from my reverie. I struggled to figure out life without Rick. I needed to start a new story. Healing had begun. Memories came back with fondness instead of tears. The train came into view. A halo of light from the tunnel entrance surrounded the locomotive as it crawled to a stop.

I threw my knapsack over my shoulder and wheeled my case of art supplies to the train. The conductor directed me to my sleeper compartment. The bed, sink, seat, and closet squeezed together with no room to spare. At that moment, I enjoyed being alone. This was my adventure. The commotion of boarding the train subsided. In my compartment, my thoughts again turned to Mary and the road ahead of her.

Melancholy approached like a storm, growing more ominous as it moved closer. Torrents of rain fell when dark thoughts threatened,

Wisconsin farmland

preferring death to life. I knew I couldn't dwell there. I knew I needed to choose between the living and the dead. As quickly as the clouds descended, they dissipated. My boys, Mary, and my brothers all expected me to be strong, to weather the storm. They didn't know what I felt. No one did. Fighting off the clouds was a constant battle.

The darkness of the tunnel gave way to the bright afternoon sun as we left the station.

On board, perspective aided my healing. The world sped by the window of my compartment. I spent hours captivated by the views. Towns and cities emerged and vanished. Distance devoured them as though they never existed. Green blocks of farmland built the land-scape, followed by boundless areas of open land. In the vastness of it all, I realized my troubles were minuscule compared to other sorrows out there.

The train trumpeted a whistle blast at every road crossing, day and night, making it hard to sleep. Roads stretched to infinity with unwav-ering directness. Train stations, ornate and plain, large and small, stood watch, waiting for the rumbling giant to stop. Crowds got on and off, strangers I'd never know. These people also had stories. As long as the train kept going and the whistle kept blowing, I moved forward.

CHAPTER 5

WATER

Water is the driving force of all nature.
–Leonardo da Vinci

At midnight, the train stopped. I had reservations at the Izaak Walton Inn in Essex, Montana. Essex is the last whistle stop on Amtrak's Empire Builder train line. Essex doesn't have a train station. The train stopped only if passengers had reservations at the inn. The staff watched for the train and picked up the guests. I saw headlights and watched a car pull up nearby, my ride. As I stepped off the train, an island of light around the tracks held back the darkness of the woods beyond. The cool, fresh air revived my senses. I desperately wanted to see more, but that would have to wait until the sun rose.

One hundred years ago, the Great Northern Railroad built a lodge for railroad workers. A couple of cabooses on the property, converted into additional guest rooms, stood beside the English Tudor lodge. Inside, train memorabilia adorned the knotty pine walls. I welcomed the isolation of no cell phone service and no TVs, Internet, or phones in the rooms.

I loved the grandeur of the West and longed to paint in Glacier National Park. The park, my intended destination, covered more than a million acres, with mountains, lakes, and streams. I couldn't pass up the opportunity to visit. Despite my excitement on arrival, I slept well in the comfort of a proper bed without the train whistle blasting.

In the morning, I asked at the car rental desk for suggestions on places to paint in Glacier. I knew to ask someone local for the three Ps: something to paint, someplace to park, and somewhere to pee. The young man at the desk understood and gave excellent directions.

After three days on the train, I enjoyed a cleansing breath of mountain air, filled with the scent of pine trees. I walked across the parking lot in search of the car. As I loaded my gear into the trunk, a woman in her late fifties, about my age, with wavy, light brown hair, approached. My equipment piqued her curiosity, and she inquired about what I was doing. I explained my painting plans and my cross-country trip.

"All by yourself?" she asked.

"Yes," I answered, unsure why she looked so surprised.

"You're so brave. I have to tell my daughters about you."

Painting Glacier National Park

It was a curious encounter. I wasn't sure what was so brave.

I found the perfect place to paint. As I focused on capturing the mountains, wildflowers, and a stone bridge, the constant sorrow of Rick's death and Mary's diagnosis faded. A stream, swollen with spring melt, gurgled and gushed at the base of my easel. The richness of the day nourished my healing.

The next day, I drove Going-to-the-Sun Road through the park. Grounded in my aloneness, tears flowed when I thought about how much Rick would have loved to see the majesty that surrounded me. Water from melting snow cascaded from crevices high above, feeding Reynolds Creek and St. Mary's Lake and sustaining the life cycles of wildflowers, animals, fish, and birds. A mother bear and two cubs appeared a hundred feet from the road. Observing life in its purest form strengthened my will to push forward and build a new life.

Back on the train, my travels opened a window and allowed warm air to thaw the winter of my spirit. The delicate wildflowers, the unyielding strength of mountains, and the power of rushing water became my teachers as I traversed the country. In my quest for renewal, the resiliency and universality of living things coming back to life after the harshest season spoke to me. With my eyes open a little wider, I continued my vigil out the window of the train until I reached Seattle.

Bob picked me up at the train station, and after stopping by Pike Place Market to see Barbara at her pottery shop, we drove home. I had fun with Barbara because we have the same name. I would sometimes refer to her as "she who stole my name." I was Barbara Benning before I married, and she married Bob and became Barbara Benning. They planned to show me around the area for the week. Nature had more lessons to teach me.

Paradise National Park, home of Mount Rainier, started our travels around the Pacific Northwest. Snow covered the peak of Mount Rainier, even in July. In the winter, Paradise receives over fifty inches of snow. Back on the road, Bob and Barbara showed me the arid eastern side of the Cascade Mountains. The high desert, with its golden hills and sparse trees, stood in dramatic contrast to verdant Western

Washington. By late afternoon, we found a little hotel in Lyle on the Columbia River. The historic hotel, along the railroad tracks, once housed rail workers, like the Izaak Walton Inn. The town of five hundred formed the perfect backdrop for our tour.

Bob wore a T-shirt that read "Pork Roll—It's a Jersey thing" with a picture of a pork roll. Anyone from New Jersey knows what it is. A blend of meats and spices, bordering on sausage but not quite, formed into a roll like baloney or salami. A perfect New Jersey breakfast includes a couple of slices fried up, slathered with mustard, and tucked into a Kaiser roll. When our hostess, Karen, showed us to our rooms, she noticed Bob's shirt.

"Are you from New Jersey?" she asked.

The conversation went on from there. Karen also grew up in New Jersey. She apologized for the restaurants being closed and described to us the options for dinner in town. We put our bags in our rooms and left for dinner. After a pizza, we grabbed a bottle of wine and went back to the hotel. The cool evening called for sweatshirts. A table on the side of the hotel provided the perfect spot to sit and enjoy our wine.

Before long, Karen joined us. The lively conversation went in all directions.

"My partner and I bought this place because of the vortex here. We both felt it," Karen said.

I had no idea what a vortex was, so I thought it best to just listen. Barbara knew how to engage her, understanding that a vortex is believed to be a place where swirling energy creates a healing force. Meditation and self-exploration are thought to be enhanced by a vortex.

Bob excused himself to have a cigarette. I watched him walk over to the railroad bridge. He looked over the side down at the tracks. A pickup pulled alongside him. I waited for him to return to fill us in on the conversation with the driver.

Our hostess continued. "He left last Tuesday. Now I have to run this place by myself. Do you want some more wine?"

"Sure," I answered.

She ducked back into the hotel and brought out another bottle. We had befriended a woman with a wine cellar. New Jersey folks are good people.

Bob returned with a smirk. I knew that look.

"What?" I asked. I knew he had something to tell us.

"The guy asked if I was all right. He asked if I was gonna jump." Bob laughed.

Between talk of the vortex, concerns that Bob was going to jump off the bridge, and a free-flowing wine cellar, our stay at the Lyle Hotel became a memorable evening.

In the morning, we continued west on the Lewis and Clark Highway along the Columbia River. Bob drove across the Hood River Bridge to Oregon and stopped at Multnomah Falls. The captivating waterfall plummeted off Larch Mountain with fury and grace. That evening we camped out in Olympic National Park. We walked along the rocky beach among the sun-drenched downed trees. Rock formations stood tall against the Pacific Ocean tides. Our adventure ended with a ferry ride across Puget Sound back to Seattle.

The sights, sounds, and texture of my expedition across the country and through the Pacific Northwest refreshed my being. I felt renewed, stronger, and more able to continue on my personal journey. Everywhere I traveled water became the focal point. Sometimes the water flowed steadily and with calm deliberation. Other times the water crashed in waves or poured off mountains. From the shallow, rocky stream in Glacier National Park to the depths of Puget Sound the persistence of water became my mentor.

On the plane home, Mount Hood popped up above the clouds as though waving goodbye. The pressures of decision making subsided when I traveled. It gave me time and space to think. Travel guided me away from the fear of the unknown and restored my sense of adventure. I learned to take control of my life.

CHAPTER 6

UNDER CONSTRUCTION

Happiness is a butterfly, which when pursued,
is always just beyond your grasp,
but which, if you will sit down quietly,
may alight upon you.
—Nathaniel Hawthorne

At home, my indecision wore on me. Time ran out, and I had little chance of another snowless winter. Frigid weather awaited. If I stayed in Peterborough, I would be safe. But I also remembered an evening at Harlow's Pub when Rick and I had watched a group of single women dancing together.

"I'd never want to be single here," I commented. Rick agreed. And yet, here I was.

After I returned, I joined the New Hampshire Plein Air Group for a painting day in the White Mountains. I started for home in the afternoon, but I didn't want the day to end. The clear sky and deliciously warm air begged me to linger.

I turned onto a side road, looking for scenes to photograph for future paintings. The road curved around an open field. An alcove of trees on the right enveloped a small white church with a modest steeple.

An aging farmhouse, in need of fresh paint, stood at a bend in the road with a large barn beside it. A symphony of gray hues covered the barn, the paint long gone. Deep grooves, etched by time, revealed the texture of seasons the barn had endured. At times, I felt like that barn—empty, broken—and of little use anymore.

I pulled over, grabbed my camera, and started taking pictures.

The field across the street overflowed with tall grasses and wildflowers, the perfect foreground for pictures of the little white church. Camera at the ready, I trekked into the field focused on the potential for a painting. Intoxicated by the sweet scent of late summer floating through the field, I snapped more pictures. Faint whispers of wings called to me. I stopped and looked around. The entire field hummed with butterflies.

Rick spoke to me. I could hear him as clearly as if he were standing in front of me. He told me he believed in me and to let go of the past. The time had come to live my life. One last time, he told me I needed to believe in myself. His presence freed me from my cocoon of sorrow and doubt. My confusion cleared. I knew what to do. At that moment, I decided to buy the house in Hampton Falls. Less than a month later, I signed the papers.

When I first looked at the house in Hampton Falls, it stood vacant and uninhabitable, abandoned by the previous owner. Signs of neglect cried out for attention. Faded gray paint and a crumbling driveway foreshadowed conditions inside the humble ranch house. The uncut lawn tickled my ankles and smelled of spring. I needed a home; the house needed me. I returned in the fall for a closer look.

The list of necessary improvements started with new windows and doors to keep out the cold and new wiring to make it safe. Nothing in the kitchen looked salvageable, not even the cheap linoleum, which tried to look like brick, or the pink Formica countertop. There were no appliances. The wood floors in the living room and gallery required sanding, but the sunlight pouring in from the front windows provided a hopeful sign.

The gallery room showed the most potential, with plenty of wall space. I stood in the middle of the room and tried to visualize it as a gallery while tempering my emotions. Confident that the room would work, I worried about the rest of the house.

A harrowing trip down the basement steps, too steep to meet current building codes, and with only enough headroom for a troll, led to the garage. The tour continued through a dirty, paint-chipped, green door into the basement.

A damp smelling room of cinderblock and cement had potential as a workshop. Conspicuously absent was a furnace. I looked up at the floor joists. A minimal amount of mechanical and plumbing connections to the upstairs sparked a thought. Moving the kitchen would be easy. That thought created a turning point. The new floor plan I had in mind accommodated both a business and a home.

Renting my home in Peterborough was easy; moving was hard. It only took a couple of weeks to find a tenant, which solved the problem of paying the mortgage. Leaving Peterborough felt like an amicable divorce. I had learned how to stack wood, care for a horse, and throw mud (tape sheetrock seams), but I couldn't stay there. I knew I needed to start my life over, or, as Rick would say, I needed an ECO (engineering change order).

The transition from a four-bedroom house to a one-bedroom demanded disposing of anything that wouldn't fit or I didn't need. After two garage sales, I had to decide what to move and what to discard. Bad paintings, frames needing refinishing, and a broken antique rocking chair started the process. The burden of having too many things lifted as I heaved unwanted items into the dumpster.

The purging felt bittersweet. It wasn't outgrown toys I was leaving behind but a composite of the family we once were. Tools suggested everything Rick could fix, the bucket of baseballs a reminder of Mike's sporting days, and hockey equipment that evoked memories of Richard.

One box I didn't need but couldn't discard sat in a corner of the basement. Time had turned the color to amber, and the smell of old cardboard told its age. I knew the contents even without a label. It belonged to Rick. Boston's Berklee College of Music required composition majors to write an orchestration piece. Each instrument had its own set of sheet music. He wrote all the notes by hand on blank staff paper. No orchestra would ever play his music. It played only in Rick's head. The sheets of music filled the box. For thirty-four years and five moves, the box had stayed with Rick. The grating sound of packing tape being pulled through the dispenser echoed through the basement as I prepared the box to move once again.

With one month remaining before the tenants moved into my house in Peterborough, I also needed to focus on the Hampton Falls house. I forged ahead with interviewing contractors. A father-son team, Steve and Kenny, said they'd bring in an architect. They got the job. I knew I wanted to add a second floor but only if it was feasible. The architect provided reassurance.

I took a break from packing and drove the ninety miles to Hampton Falls to check on the progress. One morning I arrived to find the old rafters, plywood, and shingles overflowing a dumpster parked in the yard. Kenny and his team were dismantling the roof. A gaping hole exposed the house as though it were stripped naked. A blue tarp lay on the ground, ready to cover it. My house stood there vulnerable and broken, awaiting its rebirth.

Later in the week, I returned to see a truck backing into the driveway. A boom telescoped from the truck, high in the air, with a long cable descending over the ridge beam lying on the ground. The driver got out of the truck and approached Steve and Kenny to explain the process of getting the twenty-foot beam off the ground and in place on the roof. At waist height, Kenny put a level on the beam and signaled the driver with a thumbs-up. Kenny climbed the ladder and guided the suspended beam over the center of the rafters. The workmen pounded the ridge beam in place. Once again, Kenny reached for his level. It was perfect.

It would be another week before they sealed the exterior with windows, skylight, and roof shingles. The interior second floor would be next year's project, but for the time being, the completed exterior signaled progress. The once-neglected house now stood a little taller, sturdier, more confident, and so did I.

CHAPTER 7

APPROVED

*Life is like riding a bicycle. To keep your balance,
you must keep moving.*
—Albert Einstein

New tenants moved into my house in Peterborough, and I moved into the Seascape Inn, Hampton Beach. The location across the street from the ocean made up for the lack of luxury. The reasonable off-season rates helped my budget. The inn allowed dogs, and I could drive to my new house in ten minutes. A fridge, microwave, and bed were all I needed.

The dark and depressing room at the inn gave way to Tigger's morning walks on the beach. Each morning I watched the sun rise over the Atlantic Ocean. The water continued to be my mentor. As a teenager, I walked along the beach during summer vacation to clear my head. As an adult, I watched the waves continue to roll onto the shore. The constancy of the tides reminded me to keep pressing ahead.

I spent as little time in the room as possible. I bought a desk at Staples and put it together in my gallery. With my desk in place, I set up my computer and began work on the business. The finish work on the house was my responsibility. On weekends, after the contractors completed their tasks, I painted walls, hung curtains, and installed hardware to hang paintings. With each accomplishment, my confidence grew.

The name "Color Notes Art Gallery" came to me during a landscape painting demonstration. With brush in hand, pushing paint around the canvas, the artist emphasized getting the right color note. Color note! The familiar phrase grabbed me. The word "notes" would honor Rick's support by connecting music to the gallery.

The house and I were works in progress. The sounds of hammers and power tools resonated throughout my new home as I worked, designing a logo, building a website, and developing a marketing plan. Working in the gallery, I monitored the contractors' progress.

I needed to refinish a piece I'd bought at a salvage store when work began in the kitchen. The red butler's pantry—a vintage cabinet, ten feet tall by six feet wide, with cupboards above and below—needed work. Kenny and Dennis brought it up from the basement on Friday afternoon. I had the weekend to work on it. A less expensive substitute for new kitchen cabinets, it added character. In my zeal to "make the house my own," my color selection for the butler's pantry failed. With too much red in the lavender I'd aimed for, it looked hideous. I had to paint the whole piece so the new color would cover it evenly. Monday morning, when the workers arrived, Kenny looked askance at my project.

"I don't wanna hear about it. The color is awful," I said.

"Oh, good, I was afraid I had to lie and say it looked great," he responded.

The following weekend, I completed work on the butler's pantry. Lavender paint, faux-tin ceiling panels for the backsplash, with two-inch glass and ceramic tiles for the counter. The rest of the cabinets went in next; the microwave, stove, and sink followed. Kenny slid the refrigerator into place in the kitchen. With the kitchen complete, I considered the house livable and checked out of the Seascape Inn.

To move in legally, I needed a permit to occupy, but everything in the house didn't meet building code requirements. It was close enough for me, so I unpacked an air mattress and moved in. When Mark, the building inspector, came by, I deflated my bed and shoved it into the closet.

Doubt crept in when I found six inches of water in the basement. All my belongings stored on the floor were drowning. The rain, the frozen ground, and an unplugged sump pump caused the problem. The damage, though minimal, strained my confidence. With the volume of work needed on the house, complications piled up. The garage walls needed reinforcing, the poor quality of the water called for the installation of a filtration system, and back at the Peterborough house, an ice dam had damaged the gutters. Each required another outlay of funds. I watched my money swirl around the drain, sucked into a black hole.

Kenny arrived and called Steve to tell him about the problem. The contractors took control of the situation.

"When Kenny said you were in tears, I knew it was bad. You've been pretty tough throughout this whole thing," Steve said.

That gave me the boost I needed to confront the problem. The solution entailed digging a ditch around the foundation, redirecting any future water away from the house. Heavy equipment and excavating meant more money. One evening, halfway into that project, the propane tanks fell into the ditch. The fire department came out, with lights flashing, and found a gas leak. They disconnected the tanks, leaving me with no heat. I assured them that Tigger and my electric blanket would keep me warm. The challenges continued mounting.

I understood unexpected things happen in any construction project, but it wore down my endurance. There's determined and there's stupid. The fear of falling into the latter category hounded me. This whole exercise might be the height of folly. Throughout the process, I posted pictures online for friends. That word brave kept popping up. Brave or stupid, I asked myself.

Doubt lingered when the unexpected happened, but success restored my confidence. The butler's pantry, a much-improved lavender, now looked great. The white chandelier with pink baubles installed above the sink on the island brought the bohemian style I wanted.

Wooden shutters, left behind by the previous owners, painted the same color as the pantry, added to the shabby chic style I loved. I asked Kenny to mount one as a cookbook shelf above the window in the kitchen. At first, he looked at me with a knitted brow, not sure about my idea. His expression gradually turned into a smile.

"We could use the other shutters for backing to the cabinets on the island. That'll save you some bucks right there."

"Excellent idea," I replied.

The repurposed materials saved money and gave the house a unique look. From then on, the contractors welcomed the finishing touches I proposed with my salvage store purchases. The real breakthrough came when Steve called me outside to look at the battered basement door that had been thrown on the junk pile.

"Would this work for the sliding barn door you wanted?" he asked.

"Yup, it's perfect."

When the time came, I took my sander to it, and the well-worn door became a focal point of the gallery. The sliding barn door and repurposed shutters became the quirky and personal additions I enjoyed most. But regardless of my achievements, my melancholy lingered.

Christmas was a sad affair. I tried to make it like it used to be. I scoured the basement for Christmas decorations and draped a red tablecloth over a large box in the living room, not yet unpacked. A small, fake Christmas tree sat on top of the box. An angel dressed in red velvet sat alongside the tree. I tried to make the house festive. Mike and Richard came over for Christmas dinner. It wasn't the same without Rick and never would be. Holidays, birthdays, and anniversaries all carried a burden that time eased but never erased.

An entire year had passed since Rick's death. Despite that, a song would come on the car radio or a movie on TV, and tears I tried to run away from returned.

Mike and I were driving in the car and "Time in a Bottle" by Jim Croce came on the radio. "Turn this up. I love this song," I said to Mike. And then, "Change the station, now." It had become another one of those songs that made me cry.

The spaces in between those moments grew further apart. But like Christmas, nothing would ever be the same. It was something I needed to accept to move forward. Happiness became a choice, just like sadness.

In February, I faced the Hampton Falls Planning Board. I had received notice to appear at its meeting after petitioning the town for a business permit. Snowbanks surrounded the town hall parking lot. Shoulders back, chin up, I marched across the pavement. The snow crunched beneath my feet. I advanced down the corridor, passed the closed offices of the recreation department, the town clerk, and the tax collector. Double doors at the end of the hall remained closed until seven o'clock when the meeting began.

The doors creaked open from the inside, much like those of Dracula's castle. Wood paneling that had darkened with age scaled the walls. The room smelled old, like a pile of yellowing newspapers stored in a basement. Immense windows let in the scant light from streetlights, along with plenty of cold air. The committee members sat in a row, dressed in warm sweaters and fleece.

Mark Smith, the town's building inspector, sat at a smaller table. He had been to my house many times to make sure the contractors had met all building code requirements. Four rows of folding chairs sat facing the planning board.

I was eager to get on with the process. Too much delay and the thoughts going through my brain would go from I can do this to What if they don't grant me the permit? to What the hell am I doing? I could only maintain composure for a limited time.

The events of the last fourteen months raced through my head. Nothing could justify denying my petition. My house was zoned residential, even though commercial properties surrounded it. I had read all the regulations, and I was ready.

"What are you planning for signage?" Chairperson Butler asked.

"Some flashing, bright neon would be nice," I said with a chuckle.

Eyebrows raised and backs stiffened among the board members.

"Just kidding." I knew it would be an issue. "I'm working on something four feet by six feet and ten feet from the road with no up-lighting." The regulations stated no up-lighting; that is, a spotlight beneath a sign pointing upwards.

Their expressions softened. I knew the regulations and had every intention of adhering to them. The rules about sizes and lighting were silly based on the properties surrounding mine, but I understood it would be a concern. The next question caught me off guard.

"Are you currently living there?"

I didn't have my permit to occupy yet, and there was Mark, well aware of my situation. I glanced over at him. His head hung down, staring at some papers, avoiding eye contact with me.

"Yes, I am."

"Are we ready to vote?" All seven board members nodded. The chair called the roll.

I held my breath as she called each member's name.

"Aye," "Aye," "Aye," "Aye," "Aye," "Yes," (there's always one). "And it's a yes for me," the chair said. "Congratulations, and good luck, Ms. Busenbark."

I thanked them, gathered up my hat and gloves, and paced myself as I walked out of the room, wanting to skip down the hall, laughing and singing. I threw open the door to the outside. The frigid air hurt my nose but didn't dampen my spirits. It was good to be alive.

"I did it! I did it!" I repeated as I hurried across the parking lot.

I hopped into my car, cranked up the music, and sang along with Carole King. I did feel the earth move. After a five-minute drive home, I entered my garage, elated with all I'd accomplished. I walked in the door, and it hit me. No one was there to celebrate my victory. Tigger greeted me with great enthusiasm, happy to see me. My major life event and a wagging tail was the extent of the celebration. I had tried living alone for long enough, and that night I decided I didn't like it. I needed a new plan.

The answer to happiness comes from within, but the comfort of companionship makes life easier. Independence is a fine thing, but it doesn't require being alone. I proved to myself that I could manage my affairs. Life's lessons kept coming, and I tried to keep up with the homework. The time had come to make another leap forward. I created an account on Match.com.

CHAPTER 8

DATING

In the end, we only regret the chances we didn't take.
–Lewis Carroll

The world had changed since I'd last dated. With no idea what to expect or how online dating worked, I logged on and started the process. The anonymity relieved some of my trepidation, but the concept seemed bizarre, like ordering a car online and selecting what options you wanted. I never thought about defining people, myself included, as a list of features.

Instead of asking about engine size, body style, and transmission, the dating site asked what height and body type I'd like in a partner, followed by, "What superpower do you wish you had?" Throw in the profound question, "What makes you happy?" and a mix of cynicism and sarcasm threatened to taint my responses. These were questions meant for a younger person. I sucked it up and played along.

Each morning my inbox contained a list of potential dates an algorithm had deemed compatible. Being a "Jersey girl," I was tough and determined but with a soft side, and I tried to be fair. I knew my attitude could revert back to lessons learned in New Jersey with a swift and severe response if required. Maybe living in New Hampshire for so long I'd lost my edge, or maybe I'd lost my footing in this unfamiliar territory.

After several dates, I found some men pleasant, and some made it obvious why they were no longer married. How they found anyone to marry them in the first place proved to be a bigger mystery. On occasion, I even sought dating advice from my sons, a strange turn indeed.

A computer profile and conversations in a text box have their limitations. I understood not everyone embraced technology, especially in my age bracket. One date proved the folly of my generosity in overlooking warning signs. I hesitated, but he persisted. My inner "Jersey girl" must have been asleep because I relented.

We met at a local restaurant a few miles from my home. At the time, I was still sleeping on my air mattress. A bed would have been preferable, but the house wasn't quite finished. When I got to the restaurant, my date was waiting for me by the door. We entered, and he asked for a table for two. The hostess picked up two menus and led the way.

The clanging of dishes and dinging of the kitchen bell melded with the lively cadence of conversations resonating throughout the restaurant. The scent of grilled hamburgers and fried fish rushed out as the kitchen door swung open. A waitress balancing a tray of food headed for the dining room ahead. The hostess guided us past the bar to a dark wooden booth.

Once seated, my date started the conversation.

"You know, you're lucky I asked to meet you. I've been on dating sites for two years, and you're only the second woman I've asked out."

That woke up my inner "Jersey girl."

"Oh?" I said, trying not to reveal what a jackass he sounded like. I should be flattered. He was an average looking, middle-aged man with the people skills of a flat tire.

"I'm very particular," he continued. "I saw your picture, read your profile, and found you very interesting."

"Thank you, that's very nice," I responded.

Why did I agree to meet him? What was I thinking?

Lunch arrived. I decided small talk was the way to go, keep it light. That's how it went for a short time. I talked about the weather and work. Then he headed south again.

"I owned a garage, but I had to declare bankruptcy last year," he said.

"I'm sorry, that's unfortunate."

I began having a whole conversation with myself in my head. This is not where I want to be right now. Why did he ask me out? Eat fast, girl. It's your only option.

He droned on about the economy and how hard things were for the little guy to get ahead.

"We never thought this is where we'd be at this stage in our lives, did we, Barb?"

Ah, "we"? Not me, buddy, you. "No, we didn't."

"Dessert or coffee?" our server asked.

That wasn't going to happen.

The check arrived as we were finishing up. He paid, and we headed into the parking lot. He led me toward his car, opened the trunk, reached in, and pulled out a bouquet. That was unexpected. We said our goodbyes and parted.

Later that evening, there was a message from him in my inbox on the dating site. You could call it a "nastygram." He said I should have picked up the check after he told me about his bankruptcy. He also mentioned dog hair on my coat. I thought about responding with "I prefer Tigger's company." After a deep breath, I typed my response, "I'm sorry you feel that way," and clicked send. Problem solved.

The mixture of dates became an exercise in limiting expectations. The man with strong political opinions made it clear that views contrary to his were wrong. The tall man with the pickup thought our height difference presented a problem. The man with five kids and a minivan made me laugh. A man I turned down for coffee objected, "But it's only coffee!"

The dance tried my patience until I met Tim.

Tim stood out as attractive, intelligent, fun, and gentlemanly. We first met for lunch at Popovers, a café in Portsmouth. When I approached, a man hovered near the front door, as though waiting for someone. He wore navy slacks, a waist-length ski jacket, and loafers. With gray hair, neatly combed, and a warm smile, he looked like his picture on the dating website. It turned out some profile photos were taken long ago in a galaxy far, far away.

An odd combination of familiarity and newness emerged during the first meeting. Because of the information provided in his profile and the digital exchanges—emails, phone conversations, and his description on the website—I felt as though I almost knew him.

I wore my black leather boots. The sound of my heels clacking against the sidewalk brought back memories of our elementary school principal, Sister Winifred, marching down the corridor. Her footsteps elicited fear and gave off authority.

The sound made my presence known. It's hard to exude assuredness when you aren't even five feet tall, but the boots helped. When our eyes met, we shared a friendly smile. Tim introduced himself and opened the door for me.

The aroma of freshly baked bread and bright lights created a cheery atmosphere. We made our selections from the glass display case and looked for a table.

"I'm not sure this is going to work," I said as we sat down.

Tim tilted his head and looked at me.

"I'm a Mets fan," I told him. I knew from his profile he was a Yankees fan.

He smiled, not sure what to make of my comment until I laughed. He joined in with a wide grin. I didn't care about his poor choice of allegiance in baseball teams, just his reaction to a little tweaking. A sense of humor is the most important characteristic I could think of, other than not having filed for bankruptcy.

At first, I hesitated in responding to him on the dating website. He was twelve years my senior. I had already been widowed once. I didn't want to sign up for a second go at that nightmare. Friends helped put that notion to rest. I decided that was no way to live. What was I going to do, ask for the medical records of any potential date? It wasn't like buying a horse and getting the vet to do a preliminary examination before taking ownership.

Driving home, I was glad my friends had talked me into responding to him. I thought lunch went well. Did he feel the same?

Things started to fall into place. Spring approached, and with work on the inside of the house nearly completed, focus turned to the outside. Putting in a walkway to the gallery, paving the parking lot, building a retaining wall, and painting the outside all required the snow to melt and the rain to stop. The three feet of snow that had accumulated over the winter saturated the ground as it melted.

I hired Stateline Paving and Landscape in Hampton Falls. They were highly recommended by everyone I spoke with. Luis, the owner, came by when things had dried out enough to begin work.

I went outside to meet him.

"What's your husband do?" he asked with a Portuguese accent.

"I don't have one."

"No?"

"He died."

"You need to get a new one."

CHAPTER 9

SAILING

I'm not afraid of storms,
for I'm learning how to sail my ship.
—Louisa May Alcott

Tim invited me to dinner and then to a movie. Our relationship breathed new life into my struggling existence. For the first time in over a year, I could relax. Fear and uncertainty had been my motivation. I had believed that as long as I kept running, pushing, and striving, I would be all right. With Tim in my life, that sense of urgency eased into a calmer sense of purpose. I shifted from "survival mode" to a sense of normalcy.

At first, we saw each other a couple of times a week and found we had a lot in common. We had both grown up in the suburbs of New York City; he had graduated from Hartwick College, and I'd attended a semester there. He was divorced with two grown children. My two boys were also adults. I found his calm demeanor reassuring, and I looked forward to our time together. When he said he was reminded of the Beatles song "Till There Was You" in thinking of me, I knew our relationship had the potential to last.

The chaotic emotional roller coaster of young love had been

replaced with a deeper understanding of the beauty of intimacy and companionship. But we were an unlikely pair, Tim, an attorney representing veterans on disability cases, and me, a painter with bohemian inclinations. The art world, my world, bordered on foreign territory for a man who follows the rules and reads directions. One evening, as dinnertime approached, my small grill needed assembly. Tim volunteered to help. To my amazement, he read the directions, starting with inventorying the parts. Sure, I would glance at that stuff, but he read it, line by line.

Within a few months of meeting Tim, the grand opening of Color Notes Art Gallery arrived on Memorial Day weekend, a time of celebration and a time for Tim to meet some of my family. Bob and Barbara came from Seattle to help with the landscaping. Jim and Debbie came from New Jersey with Tom and Kelly, their college-aged kids. Richard and his girlfriend rounded out the crowd on Friday night. Mike had moved to Upstate New York to be closer to his girlfriend, Christy, in Canada.

Tim and I sat on the couch and watched the night unfold, as though at the movies. The raucous banter of my family took flight. I tried to maintain some level of decorum, which fooled no one.

Debbie silenced the group momentarily with, "Okay, who wants pizza?" and then warned us to keep it down while she called in the order.

"That's right, four pizzas, two pepperoni, a plain, and a veggie." As she continued ordering, our attention strayed, and the volume in the room increased again. Debbie frantically waved her arm to try to shut us up. It was futile. We waved back and continued talking.

"Thirty minutes? Okay, thanks, we'll pick them up." With that, she hung up. "I hate you all. Except you, Tim."

We all laughed.

Everyone enjoyed themselves, even when the pizza boxes caught fire while sitting on the stove.

When the time came for Tim to leave, I walked him to the door to say good night.

"So, what'd you think?" I asked.

"They were a lot of fun."

"Really?"

"Yeah, like my family in Maine, only a bit more boisterous."

"Yeah, I bet," I responded with a laugh.

"I'll see you tomorrow."

With that, and a kiss, he headed back to Maine.

The grand opening arrived. Many friends came to show their support, but few art-buying customers. The business end of things needed attention.

I joined the Chamber of Commerce and other business associations. Tim attended the monthly events with me. I found them torturous. He'd shake hands, introduce himself, and effortlessly tell them about the gallery. I, too, would introduce myself, smile, and chat, but I required a glass of wine first. Officially, I had become a small business owner, but in my heart, I was just a painter. The pretense seemed necessary for the business end of the gallery to work.

A lovely break came when Tim invited me to go sailing and then to dinner at the Portland Yacht Club. I'd never been sailing and didn't know what to expect. I'd also never been to a yacht club. This invitation required a call to my cousin Mary.

"Hey, girlie girl," Mary answered the phone with her familiar greeting and sweet southern accent.

"He invited me to go sailing and then to the yacht club for dinner."

"Great!"

"What do I wear?" I asked, slightly panicked.

"Just think Lands' End."

"Got it. I knew you'd know the answer."

I embraced the newness of my life. The anxiety of heading into the unknown made things interesting and terrifying.

The drive north to Tim's home in Falmouth, Maine, took an hour. His house sat on a rocky bluff overlooking Casco Bay in the Gulf of Maine. The cottage had been in his family for more than one hundred years. His parents, grandparents, and great-grandparents had all retired there. Threads of each generation embroidered the rooms, connecting the past and present. Built-in shelves in the living room displayed vintage books from Tim's great-grandfather. A cupboard by the kitchen housed teacups used by his grandparents. Baby food jars lined the basement sill, filled with nuts, bolts, and screws his father had saved. His mom's cookie jar, bright yellow and shaped like a pear, sat on the dining room table.

Windows encircled the front room and presented a mesmerizing view of the bay. In the summer, a variety of boats filled Falmouth Harbor. To the left, Town Landing, with boats coming and going, and folks fishing off the dock. The lobstermen maneuvered their boats alongside the dock with ease. To the right, the Portland Yacht Club's dock stretched out into the water. Straight ahead, beyond the boats, Clapboard Island completed the scene.

After a brief tour of the cottage, we left for the yacht club. The clubhouse, tastefully maintained with planters of flowers, faced the anchorage. Bright white rocking chairs rested on the front porch. In front of the clubhouse, a group of matching Adirondack chairs dotted the well-maintained lawn. Everything pointed toward the water, which buzzed with boat activity. The launches delivered passengers to and from moored boats. The summer day, rendered in cobalt skies and azure waters, opened up in front of me as I wondered whose life I was living.

Tim led the way down the ramp to the floating docks to catch the launch. His boat was a twenty-eight-foot Catalina sailboat.

I always wondered how people got to moored boats. Now I knew. Halfway to Clapboard Island, the launch pulled alongside *Respite*. Tim got on board and unhooked the lifeline. He offered me his hand as I stepped onto his boat.

Tim knew I needed seascapes for the gallery, and lighthouses

Portland Head Light

created the perfect setting. We motored to Portland Harbor, camera in hand. Because of the time I spent working on opening Color Notes Art Gallery, I had produced few new paintings. My work featured mountains and landscapes. The next time customers came in saying, "Do you have any seascapes?" I'd be ready.

We focused on three lighthouses. Part of my love affair with New England centered on its history. Lighthouses are an integral feature of that story. The first, and my favorite, Ram Island Ledge Light, stood on the southern end of Portland Harbor. The granite lighthouse had a coarse beauty to it, battered and gray but sturdy. It marked a series of dangerous ledges, once the site of frequent shipwrecks. In 1900, after a steamship en route to Glasgow, Scotland, ran aground on the ledges, Congress allocated funds to build the lighthouse. The Army Corps of Engineers completed Ram Island Ledge Light in 1905.

"Can we get a little closer?" I urged, displaying my ignorance.

"Not really. This is about as close as I want to get," Tim responded.

Next, Portland Head Light, the oldest in Maine and most photo-graphed, sat atop Portland Head on Cape Elizabeth. Formidable rocks and crashing waves made up three sides of the headland. It marked the entrance to Portland Harbor's main shipping lane. In 1776, before the lighthouse was built, eight soldiers were posted on Portland Head to warn of British attacks. Construction began in 1787 under the direction of George Washington. Only a few places in the country reach back to the American Revolution, and New England is one of them. For me, learning the history of the lighthouse added to its beauty.

As we moved away from Cape Elizabeth, history came alive when a large schooner, under full sail, entered Portland Harbor. The ship began tacking between our boat and Portland Head Light. I took photos, knowing the scene would be the subject of a painting—a large one.

Spring Point Ledge Light followed. After the experience with the schooner and Portland Head, the squat, little light at the edge of the jetty looked like the redheaded stepchild of lighthouses. I took some photos, but then work ended and playtime began.

Summer in Maine is fleeting; warm days before July are a rare treat. This was one of those days. Tim hoisted the mainsail, turned off the engine, and let the wind take over. It felt magical. Tim's confidence shone through as he stood at the helm. The wind filled our sails. Our adventure had begun.

When Color Notes opened, I had to temper my urges to play outside. On the seacoast, the population quadrupled in the summer. My best chance of success came during those months. I adhered to the posted hours. I never wanted potential customers to come by and find the gallery closed during regular business hours. Tim respected my schedule, which I appreciated.

Painting seascapes, and working on marketing through blog postings and social media, filled my to-do list. With a background in graphic design, I also created my advertising. All of it took time beyond gallery hours. The conflict between making a life and making a living collided. I should have considered the time involved in establishing a business before embarking on a relationship. A balance between my desire to go sailing with Tim and work in the gallery required finesse.

For work, Tim required a phone and the Internet. A lot of his clients were, like him, Vietnam veterans. He dealt with clients from all over the country, explaining the rules of the Veterans Administration to the veterans. The red tape the government threw in the way would have crushed me. Not Tim. He pressed on. That's not to say he didn't employ colorful language when confronted with the idiocy of bureaucracy, but he fought the good fight.

Everything came to a halt toward the end of July when Aunt Mary's ninety-two years took their toll. When I received the call about her failing health, I began a painting of a sunrise. I wanted to paint another day for her so she wouldn't leave. It didn't help. Nothing could. Aunt Mary, the matriarch of the family, stood at the center of the Kerlin clan. She never married, so she belonged to all of us, her twenty nieces and nephews. She also represented the last of her generation in our extended family.

I waited for the phone call I dreaded. Aunt Mary left us, and we couldn't do anything about it. When I was a child, she visited often, talked back to my father like no one else, and traveled extensively. I looked up to her.

Tim volunteered to take care of Tigger when I left for her wake and funeral in New Jersey. His kindness relieved the burden of making last-minute arrangements for Tigger. After the funeral, my sister-in-law Debbie asked what I did with Tigger.

"Tim's taking care of him."

"You gotta love a man who will take care of your dog. He's a real keeper."

She was right, and I knew it.

When I returned, I continued up to Maine to retrieve Tigger and be with Tim. Work would begin again soon. With just a few more weeks of summer, I hoped I could enjoy the weather and make some money.

One month later, devastating news ripped my world apart.

CHAPTER 10

RICHARD

Sons are the anchors of a mother's life.
−Sophocles

On the Friday morning of Labor Day weekend, I reached for the "Open" flag in the corner of the gallery when my phone rang. It was Jackie, my son Richard's girlfriend.

Her voice was clear but shaky. "It's Richard. I think he's dead. He's not breathing. I called nine-one-one. They're on the way."

I froze, unable to move. I focused on the word think.

"What? Okay, I'll be there as soon as I can. I'm leaving now."

At first, I didn't comprehend what she had told me. I needed to get to Richard's house. He lived in Nashua, an hour away. There must be some mistake. I had to remain calm. I didn't allow myself to believe Richard was dead.

I rounded the corner onto Richard's street and saw police cars. It was real.

I stepped onto the brick walkway and headed toward the front door. An officer approached. I identified myself.

"This is my son's house."

"I'm sorry, ma'am, he's dead."

"No, it's not possible. I just lost my husband two years ago."

"I'm very sorry, ma'am. Can I get you a chair?"

"No, thanks."

Jackie was sitting in a chair at the top of the stairs.

"I told you he was dead," she said as I sat down on the steps.

I had no response. Being told your thirty-four-year-old son is dead takes time to comprehend. Words are flat, with no dimension or depth. They sit on a page or float through the air. I didn't want to believe the words, no matter how plain the language. Richard's death carried with it the past, the present, and a future without him. No words could convey that weight.

Tim called, as he did every morning after I opened the gallery. I didn't answer. I texted him instead. I'm at Richard's. It's really bad. Talk later.

I called Mike, Richard's brother. It was a brief call. There wasn't much to say, and I had no more information.

I texted Diane: Richard's gone. She understood. Our friendship of thirty years gave her more insight than anyone outside the immediate family. Her son Jason, two years older than Richard, referred to himself and Richard as brothers from other mothers. Diane knew the chronicles in which Richard had pushed limits and blew through boundaries.

"They're getting ready to take him out. Do you want to be here for that?" the officer asked.

"No. I don't want to see him like that."

"We can release him to the funeral home after an autopsy and toxicology screening. It's standard procedure when a young person dies from an unexplained cause."

On the drive home, my thoughts twisted around in my head like a slow-moving tornado, lifting pieces of my past and throwing them to the ground in a tangled mass of sadness. I was relieved that Rick didn't have to endure the pain of Richard's death.

The days of worrying about my brilliant, caring son ended. I wanted to convince myself it was a heart attack, like Rick's, but I knew it wasn't. I never understood why Richard did many things that got him into trouble. I worried his cause of death would fall into the same category.

Richard's first day of school set the table for years of phone calls from school principals and teachers. I didn't anticipate where his precocious nature would lead.

School started three weeks after Richard's sixth birthday. The cool morning air telegraphed the approach of autumn when I walked Richard down Wilder Street to the bus stop. Richard gleefully hopped onto the school bus while Stan Tremblay, the little boy a block away, cried as his mother cajoled him into boarding.

"You're lucky. I wish Stan would get on the bus like that," his mom had said to me as the bus pulled away. I smiled, knowing Richard's fearlessness foretold trouble.

At the end of the school day, I walked to the end of the street and waited for the bus. The children got off, but not Richard.

When I got back to the house, the phone rang.

"Mrs. Busenbark?"

"Yes."

"This is Moe LeFlem, principal of Peterborough Elementary."

Here we go. I didn't think I'd hear from the principal the first day.

"I put Richard on the bus to daycare. He thought you were working. I thought it best to send him where there would be adult supervision. I didn't realize you were home. If you'd like, I can go get him for you and bring him home," he explained.

"That's okay, I understand. I can go get him."

"Are you sure?"

"It's fine."

As I took Richard's hand to lead him to the car, his friend Jason put his finger to his lips, signaling Richard not to say anything. Jason had called to Richard from the bus window and urged him to come to daycare on that bus. The bus became a ticket to adventure and a chance for Richard to see his friends after school.

On day two, Richard once again hopped on the bus. Stan was a little more agreeable. At the end of the school day, the bus arrived, and the children got off, but not Richard.

Back at the house, I paced and mumbled, not sure what I should be thinking. Before panic set in, Richard came home.

"Where were you?" I asked.

"I was on the bus."

"I waited at the bus stop, and you didn't get off."

"I stayed on the bus. I wanted to see where it ended up."

"How did you get home?"

"The bus driver brought me back."

"He didn't have to do that. He could have left you at the last stop, then what would you have done?" My patience was waning.

"I would have gone to the first house and had them call you."

"What's our phone number?"

"I don't know, but they could look it up in the phone book."

"How do you spell Busenbark?"

"I don't know, but they would."

"A lot of people don't know how to spell it."

Is this conversation really happening?

"Then I'd sit on the curb and wait for the bus to come back in the morning."

"There are wild animals in the woods that will come out and eat you! Never do that again."

I had lost the argument.

Before the month was over, and after several more bus incidents, I withdrew him from public school and enrolled him in St. Patrick School's kindergarten. Each morning I drove him and picked him up at noon. The switch put an end to his bus hijinks.

On the way home from visiting my parents during spring break, we stopped in Ravena, New York, to visit Sue, my best friend from high school. She was in graduate school at the time. She met us on the main drag so we could follow her. Sue invited Richard to ride in her truck. He hopped in and read the signs as they drove. When we arrived, Sue got out of her vehicle and blurted, "He can read. I mean, he can really read."

Richard's life was infused with similar stories of adults astonished at his intelligence and educators dismayed at his behavior. The paradox of intelligence and poor school performance was a strain on daily life with Richard. I wanted to write all the stories I could remember of Richard's adventures and give them to him when he had a child of his own.

Now that would never happen.

After Richard graduated from high school, he joined the navy and became a cryptologic tech, assigned to the aircraft carrier *USS Enterprise*. The position required top-secret clearance because of the communications he handled. Only those whose names appeared on a list could enter the office on the ship where he and a shipmate worked. One day the admiral knocked on the door and asked to enter. They checked the list, but his name wasn't on it. The shipmate didn't want to deny the admiral entrance.

"I'm not going to tell him."

"I will," said Richard. He stepped up to the admiral. "No, sir, you're not on the list."

Richard looked at his shipmate, both of them trying to anticipate the admiral's response. They waited, listening at the locked door.

"Outstanding!" replied the admiral.

The admiral subsequently got himself on the list and praised Richard for adhering to the rules. For Richard's part, I'm sure he enjoyed being able to defy authority more than he enjoyed following the rules.

❊ ❊ ❊

The business of death is a world apart from grieving. There are arrangements and paperwork. Richard had told me he had made Mike the beneficiary of his life insurance policy when he took the job at Oracle. He said it was because he didn't feel he'd been a very good big brother. He told Mike the same thing.

On Monday, Mike and I looked in Richard's house to find a will. I opened the file drawer of Richard's desk and noted the neatly arranged papers; there was no sign of a will. Richard approached financial dealings with great care, making it possible that there was a will.

I called his work to tell them what had happened and find out about life insurance to pay the funeral expenses. After condolences, the woman told me she could speak only to the beneficiary. I handed the phone to Mike.

"This is Michael Busenbark."

"I'm not?" There was a stunned look on his face, and then he asked, "Is it Jackie?" After a few seconds, he said, "Okay, thank you."

The policy amounted to a year's salary and listed Richard's girlfriend as the beneficiary. Richard and Jackie had talked about getting married but weren't engaged.

I called Jackie to inform her and to ask about covering funeral expenses with life insurance. She referred me to her lawyer. The pain of her response reverberated through my being, followed by shock and disgust. It wasn't what I had expected or understood. Why was a lawyer involved? The lack of trust, compassion, and understanding imparted by her decision to involve an attorney in such a simple matter made everything worse. While I made funeral arrangements for my son, she talked to her lawyer.

She paid the funeral expenses, but the rift created became a canyon of mistrust. We stood side by side throughout the wake as mourners passed by. Jackie was oblivious to the pain she had caused. I introduced her to our family and friends, and she did the same for friends of Richard I had not met.

At the cemetery, Richard's friend Jared told a story of Richard's kindness to a stranger. A friend of Jared's was in distress. Richard sensed a financial problem, withdrew money from an ATM, and gave it to this person, someone he didn't know but who needed help. It showed the heart those closest to him knew so well. Jared spoke movingly while I stared at the grave. I wanted to crawl in there too.

We buried Richard in the plot meant for me, next to Rick. Instead of a headstone, I had a granite bench with names and dates carved into the seat. When I ordered it for Rick, I brought Richard and Mike with me. It was too difficult for me to do alone. I instructed the memorial shop to put my name on the seat next to Rick's.

"Oh, hell no," Richard had said.

"What?" I asked.

"We're not putting your name on there. We'll add all of it when the time comes."

I should have listened. I had to replace the seat and have Richard's name carved into it. His death filled me with such sadness. That sadness became part of my very being, a hole in my heart that would never fill, a sorrow that would never end. In every vivacious little boy walking down the street or playing in a park, I saw Richard. I always will.

The issue of life insurance created a predicament I had to address for Mike's sake. There was no legal recourse, but I believed a moral decision stood before us. I hated talking to Jackie about it, but because Richard told us Mike was the beneficiary, it forced me to start the conversation. In planning a yard sale of Richard's belongings, I texted Jackie and suggested we talk about splitting the life insurance with Mike, a fair resolution to an impossible situation. At that point Jackie ceased all communication with me, making her position clear. Money took precedence.

In the end, Richard hadn't built up any equity in the house, and the condo fees were piling up. There was nothing more to do but walk away. My past dissolved before my eyes as though it were an illusion. With both Rick and Richard gone, Mike and I seemed to be vestiges of a past that no longer existed, like ancient columns reaching up to the sky supporting nothing and temples paying tribute to gods that no longer existed.

Six weeks later the coroner called. The toxicology report revealed Richard had died of a drug overdose. The needless loss of his life, a life with so much promise, tortured me. I thought about getting a copy of the report, but Mike, who always exhibited wisdom beyond his years, said no.

"Why would you want that?" he asked.

He was right. The answer I sought—why?—was not in that report or any other.

CHAPTER II

MOVING FORWARD

The pessimist complains about the wind;
the optimist expects it to change; the realist adjusts the sails.
—William Arthur Ward

Every major life decision I had made centered on Rick or Richard, from my twentieth year to my fifty-fourth. I built the foundation of my adult life on the two men who lay buried, side by side, on that hill in Peterborough. Richard's death led me to doubt things I believed to my core. I wondered if my life was one big mistake.

I knew how to go through the motions of being functional. I had two years of practice, but I questioned my existence. Through the darkness, my thoughts returned to Mike. I wouldn't inflict any more pain on him. I needed to be strong for him. I clung to thoughts of Mike, my invisible lifeline.

Each time I meet new people, an internal battle rages. I never win. It always unfolds the same way. After introductions, the small talk begins. "Do you have kids?" "How many?" It's the "how many" part that deals a punishing blow. If I say two, then the next question is, "Where do they live?" If I say one, it's as though Richard never existed. I learned to say one, knowing that he will always be in my heart.

My cousin Mary—along with her husband, Mickey; brother Kevin; and his wife, Carol—came to visit soon after Richard's death. Mary looked beautiful. The sparkle in her blue eyes when she smiled remained, but her lost weight and a wig hiding her bald head lay bare the warfare within. She was upbeat and positive. We dined on the upper deck of the Sea Ketch restaurant with the ocean as a backdrop. The sound of the waves across the street, the smell of salt air, and the chatter around us created a festive atmosphere. We talked and laughed as though nothing had changed.

The following day, Tim took us sailing. Once again, water provided an escape. Jackets and gloves kept away the chill that heralded the end of Maine's summer. A perfect wind puffed up the sails with graceful authority as we traversed Casco Bay. Tim invited our guests to take the helm. Kevin, Mickey, and Carol took turns. Mary and I sat perched in the stern seats talking, enjoying the ride, and looking out for lobster traps.

Back at Tim's house, we warmed up and admired the view of the bay from the front room. As I headed to the kitchen for cheese, crackers, and wine, I turned to Mary and asked, "Is it okay for you to have some wine?"

She laughed. "I'm dying, what difference does it make?"

Only Mary could say that with frivolity and acceptance. It didn't dampen the mood; it was true, and we all knew it. She removed her wig, also known as "the squirrel," to show me her bald head. Mickey had come home at night, seen the wig on the dresser in the dark, and thought a squirrel had gotten into the house. She laughed as she told me the story, but the sight of her without hair made her illness more real.

Dinner at DiMillo's, a floating restaurant in Portland, brought more laughter, fun, and wine. When we were parting, Mary turned to Tim and said, "Take good care of her."

Later that evening, Tim said to me, "You don't strike me as someone who needs taking care of."

"Everyone needs taking care of," I responded.

✳ ✳ ✳

The uncertainty in my life that had faded resurfaced with Richard's death. I had Tim's shoulder to cry on but remained adrift in an unfamiliar place. A few miles from my house on Route One, across from Victoria's Kitchen—a wonderful café with take-out dinners—sat a fortune teller's house. A big sign, "Spiritual Readings by Duchess, $10 For 1 Palm Reading, Walk-ins Welcome," taunted me every time I drove by or grabbed dinner at the café. I had no idea where my life was going. I had previously visited a fortune teller in Florida. What did I have to lose? I agreed to a tarot card reading.

"Someone very close to you is going to get married soon," she told me.

"Really?"

"Yes, I'm very certain of it." She pointed to a card with a bride and groom on it.

"No one I know of is getting married."

"It's someone very close to you."

Soon after that, Mike told me of a change in plans. He and Christy were getting married in November, not waiting a year, as planned. Mike had learned the lessons of time. It was a thief. Mike wouldn't let time take any more from him. The anguish of losing his brother and father in less than two years fostered a sense of urgency. He and Christy were in love. That was all that mattered.

Tim and I made plans to stop at Sue and Paul's in Syracuse on the way to London, Ontario, for the wedding. Sue had witnessed the circumstances of my life devour my aspirations. She was the maid of honor at my rushed wedding. Our lives took us in different directions. She and Paul were both professors in the Earth Sciences Department at Syracuse University. Their work took them around the globe, researching and exploring. Every time I saw her, even with years between visits, no distance ever came between us.

Sue helped ease the tension of trying to reconcile the past with the present. We arrived in the late afternoon. Their place was lovely, an old farmhouse they had restored. After dinner in the dining room, she summoned me to the kitchen table. Before I could finish my sentence about the impact of Rick and Richard's deaths, she said, "I know, I know." Sue understood, really understood, my feelings of abandonment and confusion.

Mike and Christy's wedding took place at London City Hall. I acted as Mike's witness, and Christy's mom did the same for her daughter. We celebrated with gifts and dinner at an upscale restaurant in downtown London. The next day, Tim and I had breakfast with Mike and Christy. They sat across the table, laughing and enjoying life, their lives. I hid my tears as we exited the restaurant and said our goodbyes. We got into Tim's Mini Cooper and started our long drive back to New Hampshire.

"He belongs to Christy now," I confided, holding back tears.

The last few months had opened a combat zone of emotions, a minefield of potential disasters for any relationship. Tim's character carried him across it like a war hero in a beautifully crafted old movie. He stood by me when I needed him most. I wasn't alone anymore.

After the storm

My new life continued to move farther away from all I once knew. With Mike married, a sense of renewal took hold. The joy that I saw at their wedding gave me hope. Mary's acceptance of her life's finality, and the absence of bitterness, inspired me. The face-off between life and death kept returning to my doorstep.

Tim invited me to go on a southern Caribbean cruise that started in Puerto Rico. It confused and excited me. Did this speak to the seriousness of our relationship? Regardless, I agreed. The trip provided a break from winter and an opportunity to move our relationship along. The deliciously romantic setting gave us an uninterrupted week together. We bathed in the warm aqua waters of the Caribbean, rafted on a lazy river, and enjoyed a revealing trip to Orient Bay Beach, St. Martin.

With everything that had gone wrong in my life, Tim made it all tolerable. We laughed effortlessly, and our love grew with each day. The uninterrupted time on the cruise brought the intimacy I longed for.

At home, winter blew in with the fury of a jilted lover. As snowdrifts piled higher, it took a backhoe to dig out the parking lot of my gallery. I just kept shoveling and plunking the "Open" flag into its bracket outside the gallery door as I waited for summer. The burdens of winter became heavier with each blizzard. The volume of snow that fell made for a debilitating winter. I felt imprisoned by the snowbanks.

Given the amount of snow we received, Tim suggested we go skiing. I loved the idea. Skiing always made the hassles of snow and winter worthwhile. Common sense would dictate that a twenty-five-year hiatus from the sport would have a significant impact on my skill level. I've always been envious of people with common sense. I began my return to skiing by promptly landing on my ass as I exited the chairlift. Things improved as the day progressed, but it was not a triumphant return.

I felt like a phony. Once upon a time, I had skied with confidence. Falling was a rarity. But my legs had forgotten those days.

I said, "I used to be a good skier, really," and tried not to sound too pathetic.

"Don't worry about it. The same thing happened to me when I didn't ski for a few years. Maybe you should take a lesson next time? Do you mind if I take a run by myself?"

"Not at all."

A sense of relief washed over me. I didn't have to struggle to keep up or hold him back. By the time I remembered how to ski, my legs were giving out and turning to rubber. At the base of the mountain, I watched him head up on the lift. I popped off my skies, loosened the buckles on my ski boots, and, with Frankenstein-like steps, thudded toward the lodge.

I turned around to see Tim gliding skillfully down the final drop of Ragged Mountain's Sweepstakes trail. His graceful movements made him even more attractive to me. My future started to come into focus.

Chapter 12

Moving Together

Life is a lot like jazz . . . it's best when you improvise.
—George Gershwin

Opening the gallery when buried under four feet of snow became the norm. No amount of shoveling could make my gallery inviting through the brutal winter. An avalanche lay in wait on the roof above the front door. I invested in a roof rake. It was the best I could do.

Mary died on April 28, two years after our time together in Florida. Knowing someone is going to die and hearing the news when it occurs carries a particular sadness. I took comfort in knowing her pain and suffering had ended. She was only fifty-three years old.

There were tears and laughter at her memorial service. People got up to speak and recall the good times they'd had with Mary. When her boss got up, a perfectly light moment surfaced. She spoke of Mary's invitations to her parties and explained how Mary had often introduced her as the boss. "But we all know who the boss was," she said. We all laughed.

I left on Derby Day. The empty corridors of Louisville's Muhammad Ali Airport contrasted with the capacity crowd at Churchill Downs. Out the window, along the moving walkway, private jets lined the tarmac. I felt like the only person leaving Louisville, but I had someone to come home to.

Spring also brought good news. One evening, as Tim and I sat in my backyard after dinner, I broached the subject of our future. Endless dating didn't appeal to me, but it wasn't like my college days. Back then, everything had coalesced around plans.

"How does this work?" I asked Tim. "We've been together for two years. Now what?"

"If you're talking about getting married, I'd marry you tomorrow, but there's something you should know. If you remarry before you turn sixty, you lose Rick's Social Security benefits."

"How do you know that?" I asked.

"We should double-check it, but it was something I came across in reading about Social Security for myself a few years ago."

I was a little disappointed at Tim's response. I wondered if maybe he had already thought about marrying me. We did the research. It was true.

Knowing Tim wanted to marry me brought joy and comfort. I no longer had the confidence of youth. The uncertainty that had tormented me subsided but never left. The world isn't a perfect place, and happiness doesn't always stick around, but I had the chance to share my life's adventures with a good man, a man I loved, and that was enough.

While my personal life improved, Color Notes Art Gallery got a boost. A college student named Lyndsey stopped by and inquired about an unpaid summer internship. Her art program required it. I needed help. My election as president of the local art association, Hampton Arts Network (HAN), and upcoming summer art shows created a workload impossible for one person to manage.

I accepted the presidency of HAN, partially from my desire to draw attention to the gallery but also to shepherd the organization to the next level. The young association had been established to foster art and artists in the area. In Peterborough, I had been vice president of the Monadnock Area Artists Association which had a fifty-year history of art shows and exhibits. That experience gave me insight into growing HAN.

Lyndsey, friendly and nicely dressed, presented herself well. At first, I wasn't sure how much I could teach her, but as the weeks rolled on, I realized the business of being an artist isn't what art school teaches. Art shows, art students, and the art association were all learning experiences for Lyndsey, and I valued her help.

Sisters Maddie and Morgan, ages nine and seven, were my regular students. They were fun kids to teach. Morgan was remarkably engaged, and Maddie was a spirited, talkative little girl. I taught them how to mix colors, brought them out for a plein air session, presented art books for them to copy paintings, and set up a still life. Amy, their mom, suggested I host a summer art camp. With Lyndsey as an assistant and Amy's help in signing up attendees, we scheduled camp for the last week in June.

Lyndsey and I scoured the Internet for projects to do with the kids. When we completed our plans for the week, we went shopping for art supplies, juice boxes, and snacks. I set up my art show tent in the yard on Sunday afternoon, ready for Monday morning.

Camp week turned into the most hectic and exhilarating seven days in the brief history of Color Notes Art Gallery. I watched Lyndsey grow into her position and become more involved with the children each day. The natural creativity of the kids blossomed.

On Friday, attendees, Lyndsey, and I set up the gallery for the evening's art show opening. Vibrant jellyfish of rounded plastic cup tops, with dangling ribbons and seahorses made from paper plates, hung from the lights. On the display tables, painted clay pots, stacked large to small and topped with solar lights, became lighthouses. Paintings, posters, and fairy houses completed the week's work. The gallery buzzed with excitement as the children rushed around, showing their work to parents, grandparents, and siblings. The pride the kids showed in their accomplishments made every minute a triumph.

The week with the kids gave me hope. I tried everything I knew to make the gallery a success—marketing, advertising, attending

Chamber of Commerce events—yet I sat in the gallery day after day with sparse visitors. I could sell paintings at the summer shows, but getting foot traffic in the gallery door bordered on impossible. With Lyndsey as an assistant, I spent several weekends at shows while she gallery sat.

My tenure as HAN president gobbled up time while giving me standing in the community as an artist, a businessperson, and a leader. Whether that translated into income was the question.

❉ ❉ ❉

In August, Tim and I headed to Fenway Park to see the Yankees play their archrivals, the Boston Red Sox. Derek Jeter retired from baseball that year. The drama of playing his last game against the Red Sox in Boston created an electric moment when he walked onto the field. As a testament to great sportsmanship, the Red Sox fans stood and applauded him. He tipped his cap to the fans. I felt compelled to root for the Red Sox, but I applauded Jeter with everyone else. The thrill of witnessing that spectacle made the game a winner.

Our day at Fenway Park served as a welcome distraction from Richard's birthday. Jason, Richard's childhood friend, called to see if I was all right, a very kind gesture. I made it a point to keep busy on tough days. Guilt lingered, as did negative thoughts. Maybe if I'd been a better mother took up residence in my head. The heartache never subsided. I needed to accept that there are some things you just can't fix.

Lyndsey returned to school, and I was once again tethered to my gallery. I had good sales at the outdoor summer shows, but the gallery fell short of my expectations. It became more and more difficult to keep the doors open.

Tim asked if I wanted to go to Florida with him. Twice a year the National Organization of Veteran Advocates (NOVA) held conferences around the country. As a member, Tim regularly attended one a year. I gladly accepted the invitation. After the conference at the Disney Convention Resort, we spent a few days in Cocoa Beach. It was a nice break before the onslaught of winter.

That Christmas, Tim and I began a tradition of our own, which we kept up for several years. We celebrated the holiday in New Jersey with my family. Jim and Debbie hosted the gathering, and the scent of pine from their tree melded with a roast in the oven. I brought cookies I had made from Mom's recipes. Our trips included visits to New York City to see Broadway shows and visit the Metropolitan Museum of Art. We dined at Carnegie Deli, watched the skaters in Bryant Park, and admired the Christmas tree in Rockefeller Center. The new normal blended with the past in an ever-softening transition, the way remodeling a kitchen goes from utter destruction to the aroma of brownies baking in the oven, filling the entire house.

Back home, Tim brought up travel plans. We needed to get away in winter to rid ourselves of cabin fever.

"Where would you like to go?" he asked.

"Paris," I answered. There was no place else in the world I wanted to go more.

"Okay, let's spend a week in Paris."

"A week? By the time you get there and recover, it's time to come home."

After a few more conversations and research, we returned to the subject of travel.

"How about we spend a month in Paris?" Tim suggested.

A month in Paris. The words danced in my head. No matter where this relationship went, we would always have Paris.

CHAPTER 13

PARIS

Paris is always a good idea.
—Audrey Hepburn

An odd text flashed across my phone's screen: Your flight has been delayed until Tuesday.

"Tim, look at this."

"That doesn't make sense."

My phone rang.

"Bon voyage," my brother Joe said.

I told him about the strange text message.

"Is it snowing there?"

"No, but a storm is predicted."

"Just go to the airport. Worst case, you have a drink at the bar."

We took Joe's advice and left for Logan Airport. After a three-hour delay, we boarded the plane. Flight attendants greeted travelers as they navigated their way through the plane's aisles, hefting backpacks, rolling carry-ons, and shouldering oversized purses. They jammed bags under seats and in the overhead compartments. Tim hoisted our carry-ons into the compartment above. The noise of idling engines mingled with chattering voices and clicking seatbelts. Flight attendants closed overhead compartment doors and made their announcements. Highlighted by the airport's brilliant lights, snowflakes swirled through the air as the aircraft taxied to the runway. I longed for the plane to lift off before the weather could delay us further.

The engines roared as the pilot accelerated. We lifted off the ground, reached cruising altitude, and all pressures receded. Not just the force of the plane but everything work related—decisions about marketing, painting, and making money—drifted away. No matter what the future held, we would be in Paris by morning. There would be no interruptions, no gallery to open, no phone calls to clients, and no escaping to separate houses. The month belonged to us.

Our delay in Boston caused a chain reaction. We missed our connecting flight in Ireland, so the airline provided us with breakfast vouchers at Dublin Airport. We arrived in Paris midmorning. A forty-minute train ride delivered us to the Marais district. We schlepped our luggage over brick sidewalks and climbed three flights of stairs to our apartment.

Tim unlocked the door and swung it open.

"This is nice. It looks just like the pictures," I said as I entered.

"It's a good size," Tim said of the living room.

"Check out the bedroom," I said, poking my head around a corner.

"Wow, it's small."

"We'll see if you still want to marry me after a month in tight quarters."

Tim laughed. "Don't be silly. Of course, I will."

We rested before indulging in a romantic dinner at Le Dome du Marais a block away. Soft lighting, a glass domed dining room, and antique red velvet chairs created a sensual atmosphere. Pan fried scallops and a bottle of Clos du Château Chardonnay at the end of a grueling day rejuvenated our spirits.

In the morning, we explored the neighborhood, starting with a walk along Rue Rambuteau. Vehicles moved quickly, funneling through parked cars on the narrow street. Honking horns echoed off buildings while sirens howled in the distance.

A tiny flower shop tucked under a deep red canopy radiated with colorful blossoms, pink carnations, yellow daffodils, and paper-white narcissus. Their sweet fragrance floated in the air. The front window of an Italian market next door revealed shelves of wine bottles and hanging sticks of salami inside. A glass shelf lined with bottles of bright orange Aperol, an Italian apéritif, added color and sparkled under the lights of the display window filled with baskets of cheeses.

A fish market sported a cobalt blue awning blazoned with white letters that read La Cabana Pêcheur. Stainless steel tables offered four different types of oysters laid out in decorative wooden boxes that rested on crushed ice. Across the street, a brightly lit boulangerie—a bakery specializing in bread—featured baguettes bundled in a wicker basket. A grocery store brimmed with apples, oranges, cherry tomatoes, and nectarines nestled in bins on the sidewalk. We would not be going hungry.

The aroma of fresh coffee drew us into Café Celtic. The strong, dark-roasted coffee went well with our croissants, their buttery goodness melting on our tongues. Satisfied, we continued on our way and rounded the next corner onto Rue Beaubourg.

The Centre Pompidou dominated the opposite corner. It's the Parisian hub for modern art of all disciplines. The building's design exposes the infrastructure and reveals its systems in bold colors. Enormous ducts climb the outer walls—bright blue for air, yellow for electrical, and green for water.

In the distance, Notre Dame Cathedral's bell towers rose above the rooftops. The towers would serve to guide us there. The city buzzed with the sound of traffic and pedestrians. An ornate carousel in front of the Place de l'Hôtel de Ville, Paris's city hall, brightened an otherwise gray day.

The original city hall was built in 1535, but in 1871 Parisians burned it down. They demanded self rule at the end of the Franco-Prussian War. Rebuilding took twenty years. Sculptures of 338 famous Parisians surround the exterior. At night, dramatic lighting directed at the statues, clock tower, and hundreds of columns made an even more impressive appearance.

A traffic light held us at the corner.

"I wouldn't dare cross this street without the light," I told Tim, trying to be heard over the traffic.

"I wouldn't want to drive here either," Tim said, looking around.

"We're almost there. See, on the other side of the bridge?" I said as my excitement grew.

We crossed over the Seine, on one of the many bridges to Île de la Cité, home of Notre Dame. From John Paul II Square we stared at 850 years of history. Sculptures of saints, gargoyles, and rosettes commingled with columns, crosses, towers, and spires. All of it was interspersed with enormous stained glass windows, arched and round. The symphony of art, architecture, history, and spirituality stirred my senses.

Inside the grand doors, the church offered a solemn respite from the bustle of the city. Two rows of towering columns formed the center

Paris booksellers

aisle that led to the main altar. Eight centuries of artwork depicting the life of Christ appeared throughout the nave. Amid all the grandeur, a sense of peace washed over me. This was a special place.

The subtle scent of burning devotional candles brought me back to St. Joseph's Church and twelve years of Catholic school. The universality of it touched me when I saw the stations of the cross and pictographs of the death and resurrection of Jesus in medieval reliefs. I felt connected. As a student at St. Joseph's School, I attended stations

Musée d'Orsay Batobus stop

of the cross every Friday during Lent. I lingered as long as I could, admiring the sculptures, and in particular, the piéta at the main altar. The stained glass windows left me in awe of the mastery of the artists who had created them.

Once outside, city noise interrupted my reflections. Tourists filled the square in front of the cathedral. Across the street, the scent of fresh bread emanated from Café Esmerelda as waiters dressed in black slacks, white shirts, and long white aprons darted among outside tables. We crossed a bridge to Île Saint-Louis, the neighboring small island in the Seine. Narrow streets wound around seventeenth-century buildings. Another bridge, Pont Louis-Phillippe, deposited us back on Quai de l'Hôtel de Ville, where the iconic green boxes of the book-sellers lined the banks of the river. I delighted in all the history surrounding us.

Looking from the bridge, we observed a sign for the Batobus, a hop-on boat. It became our destination the following day.

"Come on, let's take the Batobus to the Eiffel Tower," Tim said.

Back at the Seine, Tim purchased two forty-eight-hour passes, and we began our touring in earnest. Traveling in the glass domed boats added another layer of adventure. They fit under the many low arched bridges. Pont Neuf, the oldest, built in 1578, featured castle-like abut-ments. Each bridge had a history and style all its own. My favorite, and the most ornate, was Pont Alexandre III with its gilded cherubs, flying horses, and nymphs. I loved the glistening gold trim against the black figures.

When Tim suggested the Batobus, it revealed a spontaneity I had not seen in him before. I liked it. Our busy lives at home didn't leave space or time for unplanned exploits, but Paris did. Cruising down the Seine, we were like children, carefree and curious about everything around us, enjoying our time together in a way we never had before.

We passed by the Louvre and the Musée d'Orsay and then rounded a bend in the river. Liveaboard barges hugged the concrete quays. Up ahead, we saw our destination, the Eiffel Tower, the last stop for the Batobus and a required tourist destination.

We next toured the Louvre, a place I had dreamed of seeing for as long as I can remember. We headed toward the Mona Lisa. It was easy to find with the surrounding crowd taking selfies. From there, we moved on to the Venetian Renaissance paintings. I loved the rich colors and depths of field. I never grew tired of seeing robes of red and blue draped over kings and saints. The expertly rendered folds of fabric in these paintings inspired me to work harder when I returned to my studio. The distant landscape the masters included always captured my imagination. I wondered why they included it. Did they want to paint landscapes?

The grand halls continued, seemingly for miles, packed with immense paintings. Saints, chubby cherubs, and portraits of the ruling class covered the walls. The ancient and alluring Venus de Milo marked the entrance to the sculpture area. Surrounded by throngs of "art connoisseurs" taking selfies, I tried to get a closer look to understand the reason for her fame. There was no reading of the labels; they were all in French.

I learned later that the statue had arrived at the Louvre from Greece in 1821. The French proclaimed it a masterpiece of the Classical Greek period, but conflicting stories littered her past. The sculpture's beauty, intermixed with the museum's exaltations of greatness, solidified her place in history as the world's best-known sculpture. Without her arms, no one is certain who she is because an object in her hand might tell the story. Did anyone taking selfies know or care anything about her? I think not.

More sculptures and busts, some depicting gods and goddesses, both whole and missing body parts, followed. Sculptures by Michelangelo–the Dying Slave, and the Rebellious Slave–stood in the middle of the next room. Pope Julius II had commissioned them for his tomb, but plans changed when painting the Sistine Chapel took precedence for Michelangelo. Awestruck, I walked around the statues, mesmerized by the master sculptor's work.

Part of the marble of the two works is rough and unfinished. Scholars disagree about whether Michelangelo left the slaves partially unfinished on purpose. The men appear to be rising out of the stone. Michelangelo said, "The best artist has that thought alone which is contained within the marble shell; The sculptor's hand can only break the spell to free the figures slumbering in the stone." These sculptures reflected that process with the stunning contrast between the rough and the finished marble. I had tried to imagine what Michelangelo had meant by "freeing the figures" when I read books about him. It thrilled me to see it clearly in these two sculptures. They were magnificent.

In search of more contemporary work, we returned to our map and started a new quest. As a landscape painter, I wanted to see some landscapes. Until a certain time period, almost all art was religious or portraiture because the church and wealthy patrons paid for them. We were looking for European paintings from 1350 to 1850, an absurdly broad time frame, but that's what the map listed.

More miles of hallway and two flights of stairs later, we ran into a concrete wall where the gallery should have been. After more walking and consulting, the map led us up another flight of stairs to our target. I felt like the curators had shoved some of my favorite artists in the attic, reminiscent of the late-nineteenth-century Impressionists' rejection by the Paris Salon in favor of more traditional painters.

After four hours, the maze of rooms and displays drove us from the museum. We left frustrated. I gleaned scant information from the labels by straining to recall my high school French. We completed our tour, bewildered by the experience. Having the largest collection of art in the world is fine, but it doesn't need to be crowded on every wall. We were near exhaustion by the time we made our way to the exits.

"Excuse me, would you mind answering some questions?" a well-dressed museum associate asked as we were leaving.

"Sure," I said, knowing I would need to gather my most diplomatic thoughts.

"What were your impressions of the museum?"

"The map could use some work." I hesitated, not wanting to be too blunt.

She nodded in agreement. I saw that as an opening to expand on my thoughts.

"In Rome, the labels on the artwork are in four languages. It's only in French here, so I didn't understand most of it, and I do like reading the information."

My experience with art museums spanned many cities. I was polite, and she was receptive.

"I found the layout confusing." Not wanting to say it was like you were rummaging around in the attic of the kings of France, but it was. Organizing a collection so large seemed like an impossible task, but I felt it needed a concerted effort to tame the anarchy of excess.

She graciously accepted my comments and appeared to agree. I hoped it would help. With the wondrous and awesome artwork, I thought a reorganization would improve the presentation. It seemed from the survey that the folks at the Louvre thought so too.

The Louvre was not the nirvana of art museums I had dreamed of. An overwhelming collection of sculptures, busts of unknown men, and massive portraits of anonymous individuals smothered my enthusiasm, drowning out the delicate beauty of the masters. I longed for more intimacy in the largest museum and collection in the world.

But for that day, the sculptures by Michelangelo alone compensated for the flood of nameless subjects. The collection contained a great deal more than we saw. I wasn't ready to do battle again during our stay in Paris, but I looked forward to a time when I might be ready. Sifting through years of excess in search of treasures became the challenge. It takes time to find them. You just have to keep looking. Just like life.

CHAPTER 14

LAYERS

*A walk about Paris will provide lessons in
history, beauty, and in the point of life.*
—Thomas Jefferson

Layers of emotion stacked up like a pile of old books, each with a story and hundreds of pages. The girl who dreamed of going to Paris had grown into a complicated woman. I had changed. Time and life shaped my perceptions of everything. The voice in my head that had begged to know my future a couple of years before had softened to a whisper, but guilt remained, subtle and stubborn; however, I refused to allow myself to believe my happiness betrayed Rick. Live in the moment, I told myself, and the moment was Paris.

On the way back to the apartment, we stopped at a café. I wondered if Ernest Hemingway had sat with his notebook at that very spot.

"Where do you want to go tomorrow?" Tim asked between sips of Chardonnay. "I don't want to spend the whole time in museums. My limit is maybe two hours at a time."

"I know, I know," I said as we sat outside watching the parade of Parisians. "But we have to go to the d'Orsay. After that, you can pick. I could sit out here all night just watching these people."

"We're done with the Batobus. We'll have to figure out the metro," Tim said, ignoring my comment about hanging out in the café all night.

"Planes, Trains, and Automobiles," I replied.

"What?" Tim's sideward glance was telling.

"You've never seen the movie, with John Candy and Steve Martin? It's funny."

"No. Is that another one of your stupid, funny movies?"

I laughed. "Kinda, but it's not as dumb as Super Troopers. You have to think Steve Martin is funny."

"I'll give you that, but I was talking about the metro."

"Well, so far, we've been on a plane, a train, a boat, and now we're going for the metro. It's like the movie. Anyhow, there are maps back at the apartment. We can study them and figure out how to get to the d'Orsay and wherever you want to go."

"We need to find horse racing. There are two tracks. I have to figure out who's running."

I turned and looked at him sideways. Tim loved going to the races. I didn't expect it in Paris, but it added another layer to our travels.

Illuminated by frosted glass, the Musée d'Orsay's center corridor's vaulted ceiling soared above an impressive collection of sculptures, including Rodin's Gates of Hell and a replica of the Statue of Liberty by Bartholdi. Equally massive arched windows, also frosted, let in more light. Perched high on the front wall, the iconic clock kept time and hinted at the building's origins. It, too, was a piece of art, with an intricate gilded design of gold swirling around bold white circles with Roman numerals.

Layers of history filled the Musée d'Orsay. The Gare d'Orsay, a train station built in 1900 above the ruins of the Palace d'Orsay, burned to the ground during the same insurrection that had destroyed the Hôtel de Ville. Across from the Louvre, the train station required a cultivated design. In time, the trains became too long, and Paris abandoned the building. The French minister of cultural affairs saved it from demolition in the 1970s. In 1978 work began to turn the Gare d'Orsay into a museum for nineteenth-century artwork. It opened in 1986 as the Musée d'Orsay and houses the largest collection of Impressionist paintings in the world.

The hum of joyful, hushed voices bounced around the rooms. Dark walls intensified the profusion of pigments emanating from the paintings, like Berthe Morisot's yellow grainfields, and the soft white ballerina skirts of Edgar Degas. In every art museum I'd ever gone to, I had searched for the Impressionists. There was no need to search at the d'Orsay, it overflowed with the masters I admired. Before the Musée d'Orsay, nineteenth-century paintings were scattered around Paris in three different museums. To see the works of Van Gogh, Monet, Renoir, Degas, Sisley, and more, my favorite artists assembled under one roof, overwhelmed me in a good way.

The paintings came alive when I stood in front of them, observing every line and brushstroke. Layers of broken color vibrated on the canvases as we explored the collection. By using opposing colors, the Impressionists brought energy to their paintings. Instead of flat color, dots and dashes of hues played against each other, creating the illusion of movement by blending in the mind's eye.

Viewing the multiples of Monet's The Gare Saint-Lazare, with smoke billowing from the trains and melding with the clouds outside, and Sisley's bridge scenes, with masterfully cast reflections and shadows, refreshed my perspective. The experience transported me to a time when beauty and joy dwelt together in simplicity. A time when I was young, and the paintings were just pretty pictures. The pressure of creating masterful work subsided when I studied the collection of the d'Orsay and realized my limitations as a painter. Humbled but freed, I welcomed the cure.

These artists were well known for painting "en plein air," painting outdoors. Previously, artists sketched outside and used their drawings as a guide for painting in the studio. The earlier artists painted idealized images of the landscape. In 1841, the invention of the paint tube changed everything. Until then, artists and their assistants created colors in the studio from raw materials in glass jars, making it impossible to paint outside. Tubes of paint allowed artists to create in the field. The impressionists took it a step further by completing paintings on location, not just sketching. Because the light outside is constantly changing, the artists painted more quickly, which resulted in a looser style.

I loved everything about the d'Orsay—the paintings, sculpture, photography, and the building. Even the restaurant was elegant and inviting. The quiche Lorraine's flaky crust complemented the fluffy filling of egg, cheese, and bacon. The muraled ceiling of Restaurant du Musée d'Orsay reached a height of twenty feet. Ornate gold trim framed the painted panels above our heads, with two rows of crystal chandeliers that reflected the light pouring in from the arched windows and balcony doors.

The museum's no photography rule eliminated the swarm of selfie fanatics. Everywhere we went, the people taking selfies blocked views and created a circus atmosphere. The Musée d'Orsay celebrated the work of the artists who had once been treated so harshly. The lack of photography added a sense of calm and true appreciation of the works of art.

Before returning to the apartment, we stopped at Café La Source for some coffee and chocolate mousse.

"How do you say coffee with milk in French?" Tim asked.

"Café au lait, s'il vous plait," I told him.

When the waiter approached, Tim tried it. The waiter brought him a glass of milk, sans coffee. He drank his milk and stuck with English after that.

A light dinner became our routine. We would pick up food on our way back to the apartment. At the boulangerie on Rue Rambuteau, it was my turn to speak French. The aroma of freshly baked bread permeated the shop. Decorated cookies filled the glass display cases. A large basket filled with baguettes sat alongside the cash register at the back of the shop. A line formed in front of the cashier every evening. One by one, Parisians would approach. "Une baguette, s'il vous plait," and offer exact change. I did the same using my stale high school French.

After a couple weeks, it was time for a change of scenery. Gare du Nord smelled musty. The rhythmic beat of suitcases thumping behind rushing travelers kept time as we looked for our train to London. Announcements over the loudspeakers ricocheted off concrete walls and competed with the sounds of trains pulling in and out of the station. On board the train, I watched as the French countryside sped by. I thought back on my train trip to Seattle, two and a half years and a lifetime earlier. Flashbacks of my previous life lingered.

At the British Museum, large red journals encased in glass lined the base of cabinets exhibiting artifacts from explorers, including James Cook, Sir Frances Drake, and Captain John Smith. More journals lined the shelves around the room. I wished I could pull one out to see what they had written. Handwriting is personal and would make the explorers come alive.

At the National Gallery, schoolchildren wearing bright red uniform sweaters sat in groups on the floor, copying paintings by Monet and Van Gogh. Some children took on the project with all seriousness, sitting up straight, legs tucked under them. Others sprawled out on the floor the way kids watch Saturday morning cartoons.

Westminster Abbey had been on my bucket list since high school when I had learned of the Poet's Corner. Most of my favorite poets are either buried there or have memorials. At the Abbey, several markers of famous people stood out, including Winston Churchill's memorial stone. In 1400, Chaucer became the first poet to be buried in Poet's Corner. I was in awe. Plaques, busts, and statues paid homage to Shakespeare, Dickens, Spencer, and the romantic poets Robert Browning, Alfred, Lord Tennyson, and so many others.

Benedictine monks founded the monastery in 960 and dedicated it to Saint Peter the Apostle. It was known as "west minster" to distinguish it from Saint Peter's in Rome which was "east minster." When King Edward returned from France—after being exiled—his coronation was held at the church in 1043. He then oversaw the expansion of Westminster Cathedral up to its consecration in 1065. Renovations and expansion continued until 1745. By the time we wandered through several more rooms, I struggled to contain my laughter.

"What's so funny?" Tim asked.

"Who the hell isn't buried here?" I whispered, trying to contain myself.

Tim saw my point and agreed. The number of people buried or memorialized became comical. Room after room, it went on forever. Everywhere you put your foot down was on somebody's grave or memorial.

Sacre Coeur

"Do you think people paid to be buried here?" I asked Tim.

"That's what I was thinking," he responded, with cynicism that matched mine.

The building and unending history fascinated me. I wondered if they required British children to know all these kings and queens, external battles and internal conflicts, poets, soldiers, and martyrs.

Outside the cathedral, we wandered until Tim suggested we hop on a double-decker bus. Mr. Spontaneity had returned.

"We have to ride at least one double-decker bus in London," Tim said.

"We don't know where they're going," I protested, a little nervous at the uncertainty.

"I'm hungry. We'll find someplace to eat and hop off."

Tim's prime motivation: lunch. We rode upstairs on the bus and spotted a restaurant and hopped off. The second-floor dining room faced the street below. The traffic looked chaotic, with all the inter-secting streets entering the circle. We watched the buses come and go as we ate our fish and chips. The crunchy outside gave way to delicate, flaky whitefish inside. We found our way back to our hotel in time for a light dinner and live music in the pub downstairs.

Our next train trip, to Amsterdam, came at the end of the month. From our hotel, we rode the tram to the Van Gogh Museum. Even though Vincent was unsuccessful in his lifetime, his family had promoted his paintings and exhibited them in Amsterdam. As his work grew in popularity, the state of the Netherlands agreed to build a museum for his work. Vincent Willem Van Gogh, the artist's nephew, donated the paintings to the Van Gogh Foundation for all the world to see when the new museum opened in 1973.

I loved the museum and the family's desire to keep the collection in Amsterdam. It felt right that his most famous paintings remain there. To see his work, admirers need to go to him. Compared to other art-ists' work that I had previously observed, seeing Van Gogh's paintings in person was the most gratifying. The thickness of paint frantically applied to the canvas showed Van Gogh's passion and mental state. He struggled with mental illness throughout his adult life. The strokes had an immediacy a photograph cannot match.

Van Gogh's early work is dark, following the Dutch tradition. The dark colors result from blending many combinations of complementary colors. His painting The Potato Eaters was his greatest early work. Unfortunately, the layers of colors in The Potato Eaters were difficult to view because the horde of selfie enthusiasts followed us from Paris to Amsterdam. I'm sure they knew nothing of the significance of the painting.

Van Gogh believed in the nobility of the working man, the peasant. He spent weeks sketching the De Groot family for the final painting of The Potato Eaters. Vincent sent the painting to his brother to show in Paris and wrote: "I have tried to make it clear how those people, eating their potatoes under the lamplight, have dug the earth with those very hands they put in their dish, and so it speaks of manual labor, and how they have honestly earned their food."

The Van Gogh Museum first opened during my high school years. While I dreamed of getting to Paris and the Louvre someday, I doubted I'd get to Amsterdam. Grateful for the opportunity to visit, I thought, life has been good to me. That thought abruptly ended. My inner conflict didn't let me stray far before slamming the door on my happiness. I betrayed nothing by being happy, but emotions and logic can be opposing forces.

We bought some chocolate before heading back to Paris on the train. Sacré Coeur and Montmartre awaited. After visiting the cathedral, we hiked up several flights of outdoor stairs, rounded a corner, and Place du Tertre stood before us. The Paris I had always dreamed of seeing rose like a mirage. Throughout the square, artists stood at their easels. Every day, they came to draw portraits of the visitors, paint pictures, and sell their paintings. I wished I could stay there all day and marvel at the spectacle before me.

A man walking around with a sketchpad offered to draw my portrait.

I agreed. His French accent was alluring as he said, "I can see you are a very intense woman."

"Oh?"

"Yes, you think very deeply." He looked at Tim. "He can't see it, but I can."

I was amused. What's not to like about a Frenchman flirting with you? Tim paid the man and turned to walk away. The artist rolled up the unimpressive sketch, handed it to me, and we moved on.

After touring a few days later, we gave in to temptation. Delectable treats in a window lured us in. We sat outside at La Pompadour Pâtisserie and placed our order.

"Are you really going to marry me when you turn sixty?" Tim asked as he used the side of his fork to cut through the flaky pastry of his mille-feuilles, the creamy filling oozing out.

Staring down at my perfectly round chocolate silk topped with a thick layer of whipped cream and a glaze of chocolate, I responded, "I could consider this coercion or maybe bribery. Which would it be, counselor? Of course, I'm going to marry you."

"It's still a few years away, ya know? You could change your mind."

"I'm not going to change my mind."

By the end of March, the warmth of a spring weekend brought the winter-weary Parisians outside, and I took the opportunity to get out my paintbox. Tim and I rode the metro to Notre Dame. I put on the smock I'd purchased nearby and set up my easel on the banks of the Seine, looking up at the cathedral. My dream of painting in Paris came true. As I worked, the Batobus went by, and tourists took pictures of me. I had become part of their Paris experience.

The streets above buzzed with the hum of voices chatting and enjoying the day. Music danced in the air as a crowd gathered around a man playing piano on Pont Saint-Louis. Concrete pillars blocked traffic and allowed bystanders to linger. Diners at a nearby café looked on, entertained as they drank coffee or wine.

Paris brought texture to my life—like an Impressionist painting, layers of colors, both bold and serene, came together to complete me. Paris renewed my joie de vivre while Tim made my dreams come true. On the plane ride home, I hoped the enchantment of Paris would remain with me forever. Again, I questioned my existence, but in a good way. This new life that felt so foreign became the place I wanted to be. Paris had worked its magic. I was happy.

CHAPTER 15

ART ON THE COMMON

It is only in appearance that time is a river.
It is rather a vast landscape and it is the eye of the beholder that moves.
–Thornton Wilder

Back home in New Hampshire, I returned to my daily routine of putting out the welcome flag and taking up my post at Color Notes Art Gallery. Reinvigorated by our trip, I placed a fresh canvas on my easel and threw on my smock from Paris. I squeezed piles of fresh paint onto my palette. The scent of linseed oil drifted through the gallery as I taped a picture of the flower shop on Rue Rambuteau to my easel. The north-facing window in the gallery provided an ideal location to paint.

Before I started mixing colors, the door opened with the accompanying ding-dong. Lyn, a representative of the Hampton Falls Parks and Recreation Committee, walked in and introduced herself.

"What do you think about an art show on the town common?" she asked.

"From the time I moved to Hampton Falls, I thought it was a perfect location for an art show," I said.

"Would you come to our next meeting and talk to the committee

91

about what's involved? What would the town need to do, what kind of budget, when would be a good time, that sort of thing."

"Sure, I'd be happy to. I'll write something up."

"That would be great."

Her eyes drifted around the room to look at my paintings. I loved watching people's facial expressions as they examined my work. A gesture, like a smile or an abrupt stop at a painting, told me a lot. The affirmation of an immediate reaction made the years of work in the studio worthwhile.

"I love this one. Is it Portland Head Light?" Lyn asked.

"Yes, it is." Then I told her about the day Tim took me out on *Respite* to show me the Portland Harbor lighthouses. I knew when I took the pictures of the schooner passing by Portland Head Light, I would paint the scene.

✳ ✳ ✳

Color Notes Art Gallery stood one block from the town common. Ideas swirled in my head with ways the gallery would benefit from my involvement in a Hampton Falls art show. I hammered away at an outline, including as much information as possible. If I handled this opportunity correctly, the gallery could become an important part of the community.

On the evening of the Parks and Recreation Committee meeting, I walked down the corridor with my head high. I recalled walking the same path three years earlier for my business permit. This might be a turning point. After my presentation, the chairperson invited me back for further discussions. At the second meeting, they gave me a budget and made me chairperson of the Art on the Common committee.

Perseverance, or maybe just plain stubbornness, drove me to work my hardest to make the show successful, to benefit both the town and my business. I recruited a few people, including Tim, for my committee. His skills as an attorney might come in handy.

The committee implemented a rigorous application process. We required three photos of the applicant's art and a photo of their display for review, to ensure a quality show. I made exceptions by inviting some award-winning artists I knew, waiving the application process. We had one year to plan and prepare for next June's Hampton Falls' first annual Art on the Common.

As chairman of the Hampton Arts Network and Hampton Falls Art on the Common, sole proprietor of Color Notes Art Gallery, and an artist, I felt my responsibilities were limitless. That summer, I traveled to Maine, Massachusetts, and Connecticut for outdoor art shows. Color Notes Art Gallery's success depended on my pursuing every revenue stream possible. It remained to be seen if the money would follow.

The work I put into my gallery didn't yield the results I had hoped for. Going on the road offered the best opportunity to sell paintings. Financially, it made sense. In Connecticut, the Mystic Outdoor Art Festival draws thousands of people from all over New England, something my gallery didn't do. I took part in two shows in Massachusetts: Boston and Newburyport. I entered three shows in Maine: Portland, South Portland, and York.

Shows close to home created the potential for future visitors to the gallery. I enjoyed meeting people and talking with them about my paintings, but the physical work of setting up and breaking down became more difficult every year. Tim was a tremendous help. It would have been impossible without him.

Renting my house in Peterborough required my attention that spring. I would have preferred to sell it, but I needed the income. It also kept me connected to Peterborough. On every trip back to town, I'd see someone I knew. It reassured me to think the place where I'd spent thirty years had not forgotten me. Each visit, I picked up a couple of plants at the Agway for Rick and Richard's graves. I hated moving away and leaving them.

The shortage of rental properties in Peterborough made it easy to find tenants, but maintenance issues complicated my life. All houses have their quirks. The pitter-patter of squirrels in the attic didn't bother me, but it bothered the tenants. An ice dam took out a chunk of the roof fascia. I needed chimney repairs for the wood stove to be safe. I called people for those jobs. It fell on me when the dining room and one bedroom needed painting. Tim volunteered to help. Grateful for his help and, more so, for his company, I accepted his offer.

When I stepped into the empty house, I focused on the job at hand. I suppressed the memories and emotions the rooms triggered. I had stripped the border tape of farm animals around the chair rail in the kitchen years ago. We had depersonalized everything to sell the house before I resorted to renting. The changes made it easier for me, too, with fewer reminders of my past life. I could pretend it wasn't the same place. The place where I had surprised Rick with a birthday party or where I had spent hours in my gardens.

The last tenants asked to remove the wallpaper in the dining room and paint it. I agreed. On the walk-through I saw they hadn't done a good job. When Richard had entered the navy, I'd put up wallpaper displaying old nautical maps and sailing ships with him in mind. Tim and I needed to steam the wallpaper remnants and repaint.

The drive from Hampton Falls to Peterborough took two hours. I didn't want to make a second trip to complete the work, so we brought an air mattress and slept on the floor.

Before we got to work, I peered out into the woods beyond the backyard and hoped a deer would come by. I wanted Tim to see the peaceful setting at its best. No deer came out, but the solitude of the quiet countryside resonated.

When we completed our work, my realtor held an open house. Promising results gave me a reason to be optimistic. Two potential tenants filled out credit checks. One, a young lawyer, with three hundred thousand dollars in deferred student loans, concerned me. Another asked about a dog when the lease said no pets. I wanted to be reasonable and said okay, but she continued asking for special considerations. When her additional requests morphed into demands, I ended negotiations.

Then I received a call from a new potential tenant offering the full year's rent in advance. They had cats. Would I make an exception?

We'd had a cat when we lived there. It seemed silly to turn down a year's rent in advance. I made the exception.

That settled, I took off my landlady hat and focused on life in Hampton Falls. Contractors completed the upstairs that spring. The shell of plywood and two-by-sixes became my bedroom, a bathroom, and a large closet. That freed up space downstairs to expand the gallery, but it needed some work.

Tim called, as he did most mornings.

"What are your plans for the day?" he asked.

"I'm laying down new flooring."

"What? You're laying the flooring?" He sounded skeptical.

"Yup. I put leveler down yesterday. It should be dry now."

"What's leveler? Why don't you wait until tomorrow when I come, and I can help."

I laughed. "I've got this. It's easy. It'll be done by the time you get here."

The pressure was on. I wanted to do a good job to impress Tim with my remodeling skills. The strips of vinyl, mimicking wood planks, had gummed backing. The process was straightforward: Peel off the paper, lay it down, and, when necessary, cut it to fit with a utility

Profile Lake and Mount Lafayette

knife before removing the paper. By late afternoon, I'd finished the job. Pleased with myself, I awaited Tim's arrival the following day to show off my work.

"Wow! You did this?" Tim said when he saw the floor.

"Yup. Go ahead and walk on it, see how level it is."

"How did you do that?"

"Floor leveler, it's like a light concrete to smooth out the floor so the vinyl adheres properly."

"How did you know to do that?"

"Not my first rodeo. I know how to do all kinds of things," I said with a smile.

I ordered a futon, painted the walls a soft moss green, and hung more paintings. The expanded gallery space also made a nice guest room for Mike and Christy's next visit. The previous fall, they had slept on the air mattress.

During that visit, Mike had suggested a drive to the White Mountains. He wanted to show Christy the beauty of his home state. We drove to Crawford Notch, cradled between the Presidential, Franconia, and Willey Mountain ranges. The Saco River begins its 136-mile journey at Saco Lake, just up the road, until it reaches the Gulf of Maine.

We exited the car, leaves crunching under our feet. The cool air greeted us with a lusciously sweet and musty scent. Cerulean skies enveloped the trees donned in their autumn costumes of yellow, orange, and red. We crossed the footbridge over the Saco River. Ducks paddled happily on the other side. Tigger jumped in after the ducks, realized he was in the water, and ricocheted out as though on springs. He was not a water dog.

When Mike and Christy returned the following year, we sailed with Tim to Great Diamond Island for lunch. Mike's world and mine were no longer the same. Christy was Mike's world. My world, like the Saco River, flowed into the Gulf of Maine. The cool water never stopped. It smoothed the rough edges of boulders, rocks, and pebbles. I spilled into the rhythm of the tides in Casco Bay. The place that had once seemed so foreign had become home.

CHAPTER 16

RESPITE

The fishermen know that the sea is dangerous
and the storm terrible, but they have never found these dangers
sufficient reason for remaining ashore.
−Vincent Van Gogh

With so much going on, and summer winding down, sailing offered an escape. Tim suggested an overnight cruise. The adventure of it thrilled me. Tim called Dolphin Marina in South Harpswell and reserved a mooring for the following night. Then he put on his glasses and plotted our course, hunched over the navigational chart spread across his dining table. He used a protractor and parallel rulers to locate waypoints and jotted them down to later enter them into the chart plotter on *Respite*. Tim had done this before, but charting a course introduced a new element for me. Day sailing didn't require this step.

We arrived at the Portland Yacht Club in late morning. Tim retrieved a cart for our supplies and wheeled it down the ramp to the floating docks.

"How long are you going out for?" the launch operator asked, seeing all our supplies.

"Just one night," Tim answered, sheepishly looking down at the bags of food and clothes. We'd packed enough for a week.

On the water, the salty breeze provided relief from the afternoon sun. I stowed our things below while Tim entered the coordinates in the chart plotter. Together we removed the mainsail cover. I released the mooring line, and we motored out of the anchorage around the northern tip of Clapboard Island.

"You take the helm while I raise the mainsail. Keep this course straight into the wind," he said.

"Gotcha." I understood. Straight into the wind made it easier to raise the sail because there would be no resistance.

Tim flipped open the lock to release the mainsail line to pull the sail up the mast. Hand over hand, he heaved the line while occasionally glancing up to see his progress.

"Just a little farther." I watched the sail and monitored the weather-vane at the top of the mast to make sure we were headed into the wind.

With a final yank, he locked down the line to keep the sail in place. "Okay, turn a little to port."

As I did, the wind filled the mainsail.

"We're a sailboat now. You can turn off the engine."

The soft, muffled sound of the billowing sail replaced the rumble of the engine. Tim next moved to unfurl the jib, the guiding sail at the bow. He loosened the furling line and released the jib enough for the wind to grab hold. As Tim maintained tension on the line in his other hand, the furler spun, and the sail burst open. Whoosh! He whipped the line around the winch and adjusted the sail to catch the wind as we approached Basket Island.

"Watch for the red buoy marking the ledges up ahead, leave it to port, and give it plenty of room. We're going to head toward Little Chebeague Island. Let me know when you see the day marker," Tim instructed.

The ledges, lobster buoys, and rock outcroppings turned Casco Bay into an obstacle course. The direction of the wind further complicated handling the helm. Tim's instructions were welcome guidance after hearing horror stories about sailboats crashing into rocks or getting tangled in lobster buoys. On one occasion, I'd turned the wheel too quickly, causing the sail to whip around. It took some time before I took the helm again. I gained more confidence with each trip, except for heeling, when the boat tipped to one side because of the force of the wind. Once the wind got above fifteen knots and the boat started heeling, I turned the helm over to Tim.

Lobster buoys presented a unique problem. They sit on top of the water, held in place by a line attached to a lobster trap sitting on the floor of the bay. The buoys are painted in a variety of colors so the lobstermen can identify who the traps belong to. I never wanted to get *Respite* tangled in the trap lines and raise the ire of a lobsterman.

The day was perfect—not too much wind and lots of sunshine. As we moved along, Tim quizzed me on the names of the islands. It was important for me to be able to communicate our position to the Coast Guard, if need be. There are 136 islands in Casco Bay, according to the National Oceanic and Atmospheric Association (NOAA). It was once said to be 365, which gave rise to the name the Calendar Islands. The discrepancy lies in what defines an island and whether it's high or low tide. At low tide, early sailors may have considered exposed rock ledges islands.

"What island is that off to starboard?"

After sneaking a peek at the chart plotter, "Long Island," I replied.

"Good, and that's Cow Island, a little farther starboard next to Great Diamond, where we had lunch."

"Ahh, did we come this way when we took Mike and Christy there?" I was confused.

"No, we went around the other end of Clapboard."

There were far too many islands to know them the way Tim did. These islands were as familiar to him as the faces of friends. Tim grew up in the suburbs of New York. As a boy, he would come to Maine in the summer to visit his grandparents. His mom would give him a quarter to ride the ferry around Casco Bay with his cousin Byron. I was always struggling to orient myself, even looking at the map on the chart plotter.

Tim took the helm so I could take pictures. A large yellow lobster boat, moored in Chandler Cove, glowed as the sun splashed the bow and cast its reflection on the rippling water. Behind it, a small beach came into view with lobster traps stacked on the far end. Huddled among the trees, a gray clapboard house with a white front porch sat atop a hill. I thought the house must belong to the lobsterman.

"See the red barns up ahead?" Tim said. "That's Hope Island. A Greek developer from New York owns it. There are barns, an enormous house, and guesthouses. It's for sale. They're asking ten million dollars."

"Wow, that's impressive. Their own island, huh?"

Farther along, Tim pointed out Staves Island to port and Cliff Island to starboard, followed by Jewell Island. Although the land was still in sight, there was more open water. Swells were coming from the east.

"Are these waves?" I asked.

"Probably. I'm not exactly sure where the bay ends and the ocean starts. This may be the ocean."

I wasn't sure I liked that idea, but I felt safe. Tim knew what he was doing. The water reached depths of more than one hundred feet. I may have imagined it, but the water felt denser. Then I heard a gong. I turned and looked at Tim.

"That's a gong buoy for when it's foggy, marking the ledges to port. It's green. See it up ahead?"

"That makes sense. Yeah, I see it now."

"Beyond that is Eagle Island. Admiral Peary used to own it. He lived there during the summers. His family donated it to Maine, and they turned it into a state park. A couple years ago I tried to kayak there from Dolphin Marina, but the wind was too much."

Steep granite cliffs formed a protective wall on the western side of Eagle Island. Tim kept us a safe distance from the ledge that surrounded the island while I took pictures of the house. Robert Peary grew up in Maine and started exploring after the navy commissioned him. It took several tries and eight toes, but he made it to the North Pole in 1909. Eagle Island was his home and refuge.

We continued on. The maze of islands complicated navigating to Dolphin Marina. We reached our destination by late afternoon. The grounds of Dolphin are on the tip of a peninsula and provide views of the islands. Lobster boats, ready to fill the needs of the lobster shacks and restaurants that keep Maine in business, were moored throughout the harbor. Pleasure boats filled the slips and moorings of the marina. A restaurant with a deck and a wall of windows shared spectacular views. Known for its fish chowder and blueberry muffins, the Dolphin Restaurant is a destination all by itself.

After dinner at the restaurant, we returned to *Respite*, opened a bottle of wine, and watched the bright orange sunset. It silhouetted the islands we had sailed past that afternoon. As night fell, the cold air chased us below. The V-berth in the bow was cozy and warm, and the water rocked us to sleep.

In the morning, a hint of soft light reached the portholes when the lusty sound of lobster boat engines ruptured the calm. The accompanying wake slapped the side of the boat. The rumble of the engines continued to resonate across the water for some distance. It was jarring at first but also part of the experience and the adventure. The lobstermen are not nine-to-fivers. They work when the sun comes up, or even before, and on days the fog is so dense no pleasure boats dare go out. They work until their haul is complete. No timecard is required.

We emerged on deck. The salty morning air hung heavy and cool. Summer was nearly over. Condensation covered the outside of the boat. A couple of young employees surprised us as they pulled up alongside *Respite* in a skiff. They greeted us with coffee and blueberry muffins. The aroma of the coffee mingled with the sea air.

Tigger, though not a big fan of boating, enjoyed the freedom and friendly atmosphere of Dolphin Marina. When we pulled up to the dock, he jumped off the boat. Because it stays calm for most of the morning, there's time to shower, walk the dog, and check the weather. An overnight at the Dolphin became a favorite stop for us. When the wind picked up, we hoisted the sails and started for home.

❈ ❈ ❈

The last art show of my season took place in York, Maine. All summer, I had observed how the shows were run. At each show, Tim
watched my booth long enough for me to scope out other artists and
gather business cards for potential participants in Art on the Common
the following June. Some shows I took part in had been active for fifty
years. A new show, like Hampton Falls, required marketing to both
artists and the public.

The end of summer shows also signaled a downturn in income.
I started looking for part-time work. Around the same time, friends
Laura and Ed came to visit and stayed a night in my new guest room.
They had moved to Florida and were back in New Hampshire for a
couple of weeks. Laura loved the guest room setup and suggested I
sign up with Airbnb as a host.

I did some research and considered it. When I told Mike about my
plan, he vehemently objected.

"No, Mom, bad idea."

"Why?"

"What if some guy drags you around the house, hacking at you with
an axe?"

It was something to think about. But the company screened guests,
and I could decline anyone. I moved forward as a host. It was another
revenue source, though sporadic. I needed steady income.

A classified ad seeking someone for a part-time job as a publisher's assistant looked perfect. With my years in publishing, I had all
the qualifications. I contacted two previous supervisors, Ginny, from
BYTE magazine and Ray, from Appropriate Solutions. They both
agreed to write reference letters. After the interview, I felt confident
about getting the job.

CHAPTER 17

AN APPROACHING STORM

It is impossible to live without failing at something,
unless you live so cautiously that you might as well not have
lived at all–in which case, you fail by default.
–J.K. Rowling

It took several weeks, but I finally got a response on the publisher's assistant position. I was "overqualified." The years I had spent building my résumé had turned against me. Stunned and disappointed, I refocused my attention on Art on the Common. I believed its success correlated with the viability of Color Notes Art Gallery. My gallery struggled for survival. If folks didn't come out for an open air show in the middle of town, what hope did I have of getting them into the gallery?

I designed a logo, built a website, and organized meetings. No one else on the committee had art show experience, but they knew the community, which helped in marketing the exhibit. They also knew the volunteer fire department would want to sell refreshments. By making it a town affair, I'd hoped to boost attendance. I posted the artist applications in January and notified art organizations throughout New Hampshire, Maine, and Massachusetts.

Then, winter blasted us again. Every few years, a particularly harsh winter was expected, but three years in a row wore me down. At the entrance to my parking lot, a gargantuan state snowplow took out my mailbox. Tim and I carved steps into the snowbank to provide access to the propane tank. The pile of snow reached epic proportions as each storm brought out the plow and backhoe to dump more snow on top. The fortress of snowbanks surrounding my home and gallery imprisoned me once again.

The only escape was travel. Tim and I packed our bags and left town whenever the opportunity presented itself. In spring the NOVA conference took place in Las Vegas. I couldn't resist that trip. After the conference, we rented a red Mustang convertible and traveled through Nevada's Red Rock Canyon State Park to Utah's Zion and Arches National Parks. A visit to the Grand Canyon was followed by a trip down Route 66 where we ate lunch at the Roadkill Cafe. Life with Tim was becoming a series of adventures. His easygoing and curious nature made it a pleasure to explore new places with him.

The Art on the Common committee pressed on. We put together a marketing plan. I leveraged my status as an advertiser and persuaded the publisher of Hampton Falls magazine to give Art on the Common both the cover photo and lead article. Advertisers financed the magazine. Every household in Hampton Falls received a copy. The town bulletin board, on the common facing Route One, advertised the show. I sent press releases to area newspapers. We ran ads everywhere we could think of. We were ready.

Art on the Common was a gut punch. The artists exhibited exceptional work, but the number of visitors fell short of expectations, especially among the residents of Hampton Falls. I knew many of the artists personally, and I'd asked them to take a chance with me on this new show, and they did. For that reason, I felt good about Art on the Common. I did the best I could. It didn't seem to matter how hard I tried. My efforts in Hampton Falls didn't net the results I needed. In my head, I linked Color Notes Art Gallery with Art on the Common. I needed some introspection.

I put my house in Peterborough back on the market when the lease ended. I received regular income from renting it and regular headaches too. The time to sell and move on with my life had arrived.

As summer wound down, Tim suggested a two-day cruise to Boothbay Harbor. We spent our first night at The Dolphin. After our blueberry muffins and coffee, morning found us lingering around the dock, waiting for the wind to pick up. Without a breeze, there is no sailing.

Tim saw a red trawler-style boat docked in a slip. It didn't appear occupied, so Tim peered in the window. Ruth, a petite lady with gray hair, opened the door to the cabin and invited Tim on board. Before entering, he came to get me so I, too, could have a look.

Inside, at the galley table, Herb sat with a laptop computer and charts laid out in front of him. No sooner had Ruth introduced Herb when he announced, "I'll be ninety-eight in three days." That impressed us. It got even better when he informed us that they had come from Florida on the boat and were traveling around Maine for the summer. I hung my head in shame for thinking a two-day boat trip was adventurous.

Tidy, with nothing out of place, their boat felt cozy without being cramped. It accommodated the conveniences of home and a plethora of technology, including the laptop, iPad, and navigational systems. Meeting Herb and Ruth and seeing their trawler planted a seed.

The wind picked up, making it time to hoist the sails and be on our way. After one last Tigger walk, we were off again. We were never far from shore until the last leg before heading into Boothbay Harbor. I heard a strange sound while at the helm. At first, I thought it was the engine. I heard it again and turned my head. In the distance, the broad spray of a humpback whale shot into the air. It was unmistakable.

I was thrilled at being able to see such a sight. I'd been on whale watches in the past, but not like this. The spray of water, even from a distance, brings to the fore the richness of life that lies beneath the surface. It pleased me to know we were far enough away so there would be no close encounters. *Respite* was much smaller than whale-watching boats.

Tim took the helm as we entered the busy harbor. He pulled up to the dock at Boothbay Harbor Yacht Club. We needed to get Tigger to shore for a walk before we did anything else; however, the dockmaster informed us we couldn't stay at the dock for a dog walk. We had to moor the boat. After dinner, we boarded *Respite* and watched the sunset turn the sky bright orange, my favorite part of boat trips. The world goes quiet, and only the peaceful sound of lapping water remains. The sky filled with stars as the sun disappeared below the horizon.

In the morning, the weather report told of an approaching storm. We changed our plans and left early to motor home ahead of the storm. Tigger, the not-so-seaworthy dog, found the conditions difficult. The waves pushed *Respite* around enough to throw him off balance.

A couple of five-foot waves crashed against the hull, throwing sea spray across the deck. The gray sky continued to grow darker, but the rain held off. I thought of Herb and Ruth's red trawler, whose cabin protected them from inclement weather. We made it home without incident, but Tigger and I were eager to get paws and feet onto dry ground.

Back home in Hampton Falls, I squeezed in some beach time before opening the gallery the following day. As summer faded, I realized winter had finally conquered me. I sat on the beach and stared out at the water. I had moved to the seacoast because I love the beach and the ocean, but I refused to go in the water. In New Hampshire, the water is always cold, the kind that takes your breath away. And then there's winter. My thoughts skipped over fall and went straight to winter. I loved fall. In Peterborough, the luminous colors transformed the woods into a land of enchantment. That didn't matter: winter would follow fall. It always did.

I decided to move to Florida. I remembered stopping in the town of Gulfport when I'd visited Florida with my cousin Mary. It was such a cool place. I knew could live there. It seemed like a snap decision, but it was years in the making. I was done with blizzards, driving in the snow, and weeks of damp, gray days. The last several winters had buried me. In my thirty-five years in New Hampshire, I had shoveled more snow than I could measure, split and stacked wood for the stove, and at times dressed in so many layers I felt like a stuffed toy wad-dling around in a cartoon.

I left the beach, determined to avoid another winter, and began an online house search. Real estate prices in New Hampshire exceeded those in Florida. With that much of a difference, it was a viable plan.

But what about Tim?

As closing time approached at the gallery, I knew Tim would arrive soon. How will I tell him I want to move to Florida? I paced the floor, thinking about how to broach the subject. By the way, Tim, or How about it, or I can't take it anymore. For all I knew, he might love the idea. I made meatloaf. It was one of his favorites. If he needed con-vincing, meatloaf would help cajole him. Anything too fancy would be an obvious ploy.

The light outside dimmed. I heard Tim's car pull into the parking lot, then the car door. He plucked the welcome flag from its bracket and opened the door, detonating the ding-dong signal of a visitor to the gallery. Tigger ran to greet him before I had a chance, as though it was Tigger that Tim came to see. The familiar aroma of meatloaf filled the house as sizzling sounds emanated from the oven.

"Something smells good," he said.

I smiled.

As we sat down for dinner, I blurted out, "I'm moving to Florida. You wanna come?"

"Sure." Tim was more focused on the meatloaf than our conversation.

I returned with, "Great, I was looking online at houses in Gulfport, a cool town we found when I went to Florida with Mary."

Tim's head jerked up. "Whoa, what? When were you thinking of moving?"

"Before winter."

Here we go.

"Oh." He shifted gears, and a puzzled look stared back at me.

"I'll put my house on the market and find something I can afford. My house in Florida for winter and your house in Maine for summer."

He looked pensive. I couldn't tell what he was thinking.

"I won't need to do much to get the house ready with all the work I had done."

Once the surprise wore off, he began considering the idea.

"I've always said I want to get out of the Northeast before I fall on the ice and break something," Tim mused. "One winter, there were four people from the boat club who fell on ice and broke bones."

"Richard broke his ankle a few years ago. He fell on the ice on the way to his car. You don't have to be old to break your bones."

"My friends Dick and Susan have been telling me for years I should move down there. They moved to Naples almost fifteen years ago and love it."

This is more promising than I'd expected.

"But, what about the gallery?"

CHAPTER 18

ENGAGED

When you get into a tight place and everything goes against you,
till it seems as though you could not hang on a minute longer,
never give up then, for that is just the place and time that the tide will turn.
—Harriet Beecher Stowe

"Yeah, about the gallery," I replied, my mood deflated. It was a sore subject. Success had eluded me. When I began remodeling the house and establishing a gallery, I had high hopes. For four years, I'd done everything I could to make it work, including taking in guests as an Airbnb. My only steady income came from a group of homeschoolers. I was their art teacher. It didn't amount to much, but I was glad to have the work.

"It's not working. Nobody comes in here. I make more money from Airbnb."

Tim empathized with my plight. He often commented on how hard I worked on both the gallery and at painting. Before meeting me, he didn't know how much time, thought, and practice went into a painting. He told me my tenaciousness impressed him despite the lack of customers coming into the gallery. When he saw how his question had affected me, his tone softened.

"Maybe we should go down and look at a few places."

I agreed. It seemed like a reasonable next step.

In the morning Tim announced, "Before we go to Florida, we need to get you an engagement ring."

"Okay. Where do you want to go?"

"The Jewelers Building in Boston. I was looking into it, and we can make an appointment to look at some rings."

"Sure. That would be fun."

Tim made an appointment with a retail jeweler, and we drove to Downtown Crossing in Boston. The appointment didn't go well. Neither one of us liked the salesperson. He was pushy, a little too slick. We decided to explore more of the building. Most businesses weren't open to the public. We wandered into one shop and were told they didn't sell retail.

Across the hall, a small woman in another shop saw us exit the wholesale business, frantically waved her arms, and called out to us.

"Are you looking for something?"

We approached, and Tim said, "Yes, we're looking for an engagement ring."

"I can help with that. What style were you looking for?"

She pulled out a tray of rings for me to look at. "We've had this shop for fifty years. My father had it before me."

"I like art deco," I told her.

"Hmm." With that, she slid the tray back under the glass case and reached for a binder of photographs.

"Look through here, and show me what you like."

After pointing to a few and telling her what I liked about them, she lit up, turned around, and reached into another drawer.

"This is from an estate sale. I'm not sure how old it is, but we can put in new stones and fix it up for you."

I loved it as soon as she presented it to me. Delicate filigree filled with tiny diamonds surrounded the setting for a square stone. The ring sparkled under the shop lights.

"I'll go get some diamonds across the hall," she said, smiling. "You can't, but I can, and you can pick the one you like."

"I was thinking of a sapphire," I told her.

"Very nice. I'll go get some sapphires then."

Tim and I looked at each other as she hurried off across the hall. Her cheerful, animated nature caught us off guard, but we liked the way she listened to what I wanted.

She returned with the stones and placed them on a velvet mat for us to examine. She handed Tim a loupe and explained what to look for.

The whole experience was unlike anything I had known. The idea that she could walk across the hall and come back with a fistful of gems left me shaking my head. I picked a square sapphire. Tim discussed the business end of things, and we left the shop with the agreement that the ring would be mailed to us when the work was completed.

Several weeks later, it arrived, shiny and glimmering in the sunlight. Tim slid the ring onto my finger. We were officially engaged.

By late fall I had an offer on my house in Peterborough. We flew down to Florida in November to scout out the real estate market. As we looked at each house, we tried to picture ourselves working and living there. The houses I could afford were small. I needed studio space, and Tim needed room for an office. After looking at close to a dozen houses, one stood out. It was across the street from the city marina in Gulfport and Clam Bayou Nature Preserve. It had enough room for both of us, but the price reflected the extra space.

"I'm not going to get that much for my house," I told Tim.

"I'll help pay for it. We'll take out a mortgage. Interest rates are low, and we need the extra room."

Our return home to New England's gray and dreary skies prompted us to make an offer. The closing date was February 7.

I listed my home in Hampton Falls. Within a couple of months, I had competing offers. A great weight lifted when I closed the gallery. I was weary of the fight and the intense amount of effort running a business required. It wasn't a failure. I had tried, and that is all anyone can do. If I had never tried at all, that would be a failure. I was proud of all I'd accomplished.

We moved in the middle of February. I watched the loaded moving truck pull out of the driveway from the gallery window. My footsteps echoed in the empty rooms as I took a last look around. My emotions bounced from nostalgia to excitement about our new chapter. The house looked a lot better than when I'd found it, and I felt better too. This little house and I were rehabilitated. In a few days, the cleaning crew would come by and remove all traces of me.

Four days later, Tim and I pulled into the driveway of our new home in Gulfport. The transition from owning separate houses to buying one together proceeded almost without notice. The degree of separation of having my own home no longer had any value for me. In the four years since we'd met, Tim had become my lover, friend, travel companion, and confidant. We spent most of our time together, either at the cottage in Maine or at my house on days the gallery was open. Our lives together moved forward with ease.

It snowed the morning we left New Hampshire. Gulfport greeted us with sunny weather. Winter was over forever. The moving truck showed up the next day, and the unpacking began.

It wasn't hard to get acclimated. We started each day by taking Tigger for a walk in Clam Bayou Nature Preserve, next to the marina. The boats were always a topic of conversation. The names were fun to read, and the size and condition of each were noted. How often they went out or didn't go out also interested us.

Somewhere between Herb and Ruth's trawler and Gulfport Marina, a crazy idea had turned into a fantastic plan.

Tim pointed to a boat in the marina. "If we had a boat like that, we could cruise down to the Keys or even do the Great American Loop."

"What's the Great American Loop?" I asked.

"It's a water route, down the Intracoastal Waterway, around the tip of Florida, to the Gulf of Mexico, then up the Mississippi. I'm not sure of the exact route."

"That's pretty cool."

From then on, we started reading more about it. The more I read, the more intrigued I became. Our morning walks, seeing the boats in the marina every day, helped fuel the idea. Even without traveling the loop, going on long-distance cruises cranked up my imagination. I pictured us going to different places and living aboard the boat for weeks at a time.

"Could we really do something like that?" I asked on our walk.

"We can at least look into it and decide if it's something we want to do."

After a few months, it was time to go back to the cottage in Maine. Before we left, I received a call about the women's sailing class at the Portland Yacht Club. With the sailing Tim and I did, a lot of things were familiar, but I needed instruction to tie it all together.

After I completed the class, Tim charted a course to Boothbay Harbor and Rockland. Because it would be an extended trip, Tigger stayed home with our friends Megan and Derek.

The first two days, the wind carried us steadily and swiftly. With my newfound knowledge, I worked at adjusting the sails in small increments, trying to get more speed from the wind. I loved seeing the difference minor adjustments could make. The warmth of the sun on my face and the sound of the water splashing against the hull filled me with joy.

Upon entering Boothbay Harbor, I tried to furl the jib. It didn't go well. The graceful way the wind filled the sail became a loud and frightening event when it whipped around uncontrollably. It wounded my confidence. Tim turned on the engine, dropped the mainsail, and headed to the closest mooring. The jib fought Tim as he tried to furl it. He realized the furler was malfunctioning. With more effort than it should have taken, Tim wrapped up the jib and tied it down. It restored my confidence to know the problem wasn't my incompetence. We continued on to the marina where we reserved a mooring for the night.

In the summer, Boothbay Harbor is a scenic, lively place with a mix of working and pleasure boats of every size and configuration. Restaurants and gift shops surround the harbor. Moored lobster boats hover near floating docks stacked with lobster traps. Our Lady Queen of Peace, a stately white church on a hill, overlooks the anchorage. The chimes ring on the hour. The steeple served as a navigational marker before the days of GPS. As with many coastal New England towns, the church is a prominent part of the landscape, offering protection for those who go out to sea and comfort for those whose loved ones never come home.

Currently a vacation town, Boothbay reinvented itself many times. It started as a fishing village in the early 1600s. Europeans came to the Gulf of Maine for the abundant supply of cod and haddock. The first settlers abandoned the area, claiming the winters made it "uninhabitable." I concur. Soon after that, they started coming back to harvest the tall pines for ship masts. Farming and shipbuilding grew in the region. By the 1800s, steamers brought vacationers up from the cities to spend summers in the cool Maine air.

Tim let me off at the town dock, motored *Respite* to the mooring, and then rowed back in the dinghy. We dined on tender lobster dripping with drawn butter. The dinghy dock, situated behind the restaurant, awaited. Climbing into the small craft to get from shore to *Respite* tested my fortitude. On previous trips, the marinas offered a launch or tender service. I avoided the dinghy. My fearlessness did not include small rubber boats. Bolstered by the wine I had with dinner, I sucked it up and hopped aboard the wee craft. It had been a fine day, a beautiful sail, a leisurely walk around town, and a fresh seafood dinner. I didn't want to spoil it by balking at a trip in the dinghy.

Back on board *Respite*, we grabbed our sweatshirts, opened a bottle of wine, and watched the sunset. The illuminated church steeple provided the backdrop. The breeze carried hints of fried seafood in the salty air. Strings of lights around outdoor dining rooms cast reflections on the water that bounced rhythmically on the receding tide. The joyful timbre of voices floated across the harbor. Day two of our cruise was ending in the cool breezes of twilight.

The morning unfolded, soft and gray. Distant sounds of lobster boats floated across the harbor, their wakes just a ripple by the time they reached *Respite*. Tim turned on the weather radio as I looked around for coffee mugs. That's when the words "small craft advisory" came belching from the radio. Tim and I looked at each other.

CHAPTER 19

PUTTING THE PIECES TOGETHER

Do not be like the cat who wanted a fish
but was afraid to get his paws wet.
–William Shakespeare

"Rockland is going to have to be put off for this trip," Tim said, disappointed at the change in plans.

"What do we do now?" I asked.

"We'll need to take an inland route home."

"Can't we just stay here another night?"

"We only reserved the mooring for one night. I'm sure someone else booked it for tonight. Hand me the chart that says Boothbay Harbor."

Tim spread out the unwieldy paper, its far side curling under the edge of the galley table.

"Can you check the tide?" Tim asked as he ran his finger along our route. "We'll have to go through Townsend Gut to get to the Sheepscot River, cross that, and go through Lower and Upper Hell Gate, then up the Sasanoa River to get to the Kennebec River. We can spend the night at the Kennebec Tavern and Marina and get diesel there. We'll never get through Upper Hell Gate in low tide."

As he spoke, I grabbed my phone to check the tides. "It's high tide now."

"We need to get going."

An inland route provided the safest alternative, but *Respite* needed at least six feet of water. Breakfast became a couple of granola bars. Tim turned on the ignition while I threw off the mooring line. The overcast sky threatened rain. It was slow going to stay in the channels, but there were seals and osprey and even a bald eagle to photograph as we made our way through the shallow water and narrow passages. Tim manned the helm. Navigating these waters exceeded my pay grade.

All was going well until Tim said, "Are we going to make it?"

Startled at the question, I lowered my camera and looked up at the approaching fixed metal bridge, then up the mast.

Max Wilder Memorial Bridge stood in front of us like a portal to another world. On either side, tall grasses lined the riverbanks, and deep green pines filled in the background. Gray skies allowed little light to penetrate the woods. Below us, the water reflected the dark foliage. The bridge's roadbed and arched superstructure formed the top of the gateway. Through the opening, light flooded the open water of the Kennebec River, and we could see Bath Iron Works and massive navy ships. Passing through it meant we didn't need to worry about water depth and bridge heights anymore.

Tim stared up at the height of the bridge.

"What do you mean, are we going to make it? I don't know, I can't tell!" I responded.

"You're an artist. You should be able to judge these things. Find the manual. It should be below on the right side."

Tim's smirking aside, I tried not to panic. I fumbled through the binder containing all the information about *Respite*. Tim turned the boat around to buy time while we assessed the situation.

"I can't find anything in here," I said. "Give me the waterway guide; you look through the manual."

I knew my way around the waterway guide. I could find out the height of the bridge. We used it to look for marinas with diesel fuel. We had to make it under this bridge. The height was in the guide somewhere amid the cluttered chitchat of marina and restaurant recommendations.

"I found it. The bridge is fifty feet high," I announced.

"Good. The mast is forty-one feet."

I held my breath while Tim slipped *Respite* under the bridge, its green trusses crisscrossed above. We remained silent until the mast cleared. Our collective exhale could have filled the mainsail.

Once on the Kennebec, curiosity took hold, and we maneuvered back and forth in front of Bath Iron Works. Posted signs read, Warning: Restricted Area. I wondered what would happen if we ventured inside the five-hundred-yard perimeter. Were people watching?

Three blue cranes reached high into the sky, and two large navy vessels sat in the water beneath them. One ship looked like something from a science fiction movie. The cold, gray steel sides grew wider as they sloped down to the waterline, sleek and foreboding. I posted a picture on Facebook, wondering if that would get me in trouble. Before long, our friend Paul, a fellow Mainer and Air Force veteran, responded to my post. It was a Zumwalt class stealth destroyer and cost a mere 7.5 billion dollars.

The Kennebec River has a long history of shipbuilding. Since 1884, Bath Iron Works built navy vessels, commercial craft, and private yachts. An ample supply of wood and the river combined to produce a thriving shipbuilding industry for years. The colonists of Popham Colony built the first oceangoing boat in America at the mouth of the Kennebec in 1607.

After we snooped around, we headed to the Kennebec Tavern and Marina on the other side of the Sagadahoc Bridge. Unfortunately, the Kennebec Marina didn't have diesel fuel, but we were safe from the small craft warning. All would be well . . . or so we thought.

Morning came, we tied up to the town dock, and off we went in search of breakfast. It was chilly and gray. A hearty breakfast with homemade corned beef hash fueled my dwindling reserves, and now we had to do the same for *Respite*.

The tide was against us. Low on diesel and looking for a marina, we felt the gray weather turn into drizzle. Tim sent me below to get his rain gear. I used an app on my phone to try to locate fuel but had no luck. Running against the tide had sucked up fuel faster than usual and cut down on our speed. The gas gauge needle bounced around, unable to calculate such a small quantity.

A steady rain fell. I tried to stay positive. The mouth of the river and Casco Bay lay ahead, but navigating this section was precarious. Multiple warnings in the cruising guide concerned me, but Tim was familiar with these waters. The narrow channel funneled the tidal water up into the river with more velocity than we'd already been fighting. Ledges and small islands turned the route into an obstacle course as the rain continued to intensify.

Tim skillfully maneuvered around Bay Point, Pond Island Shoal, and Sequin Ledges. Once we passed Sequin Island Lighthouse, we were clear of the danger area. We had made it to Casco Bay.

"We're going to be a sailboat for a while," Tim declared, concerned we didn't have enough fuel to make it home.

My optimism declined, the rain increased, and raw air seeped into my bones. We raised the sails and moved along well for a while. I stayed outside in the cockpit with Tim, though the dry space below called to me. It seemed the least I could do, to keep him company, given my lack of ability to do anything more helpful. From time to time, I ducked below for a reprieve from the rain.

The wind died, making it slow going. With our diminished speed, we continued getting wetter by the minute. A motorboat went by, traveling in the opposite direction, farther out in the bay. I focused on the enclosed cabin and brisk speed they were traveling. At that moment, with rain dripping off the visor of my hood, the charm and beauty of sailing faded.

Without knowing if we had enough fuel to make it home, Tim fired up the engine when we passed Eagle Island. Before the gauge registered empty, Falmouth anchorage came into view. The rain ended. It looked as though the sun might come out. The last clasp on the sail cover secured, Tim picked up the radio.

"PYC, PYC, this is *Respite* calling for pickup."

Chuck answered the call and brought the launch alongside.

"Are we glad to see you!" I said to Chuck.

"Not good sailing weather, huh." Chuck laughed at my whining. As a seasoned sailor, he knew adverse weather was to be expected.

"We need to get you some rain gear," Tim said as the launch pulled up to the dock.

"There's a thought. This little rain jacket wasn't very useful," I replied.

The long-forgotten feeling from my childhood of squishy sneakers came flooding back. My saturated jeans made lead weights of my legs as I climbed out of the launch onto the floating docks and up the metal ramp to solid ground.

A hot shower revived me, but visions of motorboats still danced in my head, along with Ruth, Herb, and their red trawler. The dense clouds that had escorted us home thinned and allowed some daylight to peek through. The freshly washed air brought out the sweet scents of wet grass and saturated soil. By early evening, openings in the clouds shepherded gossamer streams of yellow and orange light down onto Casco Bay for a glorious sunset.

The light flowing through holes in the clouds always brought thoughts of loved ones.

"Doesn't that light look like a pathway up to heaven?" I'd asked my mother long ago when the streams of light shone through the clouds.

"That's a beautiful thought," she'd responded.

Over the years, that memory came back every time the setting sun poured down between the clouds. Many more loved ones had taken the path to heaven since that conversation. I remembered them all as I stared out the window of the cottage. Tim joined me and then diverted my attention to the water dripping from the ceiling.

"I've gotta sell this place," he said, staring at the fresh leak in the ceiling. "I've spent hundreds—no, thousands—to repair that leak. One guy said it was the window upstairs, another said it was the roof."

"I know," I said.

Repairs, maintenance, and taxes were a burden. Tim struggled with the decision, and I wanted to support whatever he decided.

CHAPTER 20

EXTRA INNINGS

There are a lot of mysterious things about boats, such as
why anyone would get on one voluntarily.
–P. J. O'Rourke

A few weeks later, our nomadic ways brought us back to Florida. Consumed with thoughts of the ICW and The Great Loop, we spent the winter reading, going to boat shows, and taking a boating course with the Coast Guard. Tim had taken the course years ago but came with me for a refresher. He completed the homework in a timely manner, week to week, while I thumbed through the chapter an hour before class.

The boat shows helped us better understand what we wanted. My requirements were few: a decent bed, sufficient counter and storage space in the galley, and enough outside area to enjoy the weather. By the time we headed back to Maine in late spring, we had narrowed our choice to Ranger Tugs. Tim scoured the classified ads in boating magazines, newspapers, and online.

I gained more confidence with another boating class in Maine, America's Boating Club's "Second in Command." The two-part class:

What to do if the first in command is incapacitated, and anchoring and docking. I earned a second certificate.

Within a few weeks of arriving in Maine, Tim found a five-year-old, thirty-one-foot Ranger Tug with a flybridge at Winter Island Boat Yard in Salem, Massachusetts. As with real estate ads, online boat ads have a lot of photos. After looking at the photos over and over, we made an appointment to see the boat.

While Salem is best known for the Salem Witch Trials of 1692, British immigrants came from nearby Cape Ann in 1626. Winter Island once housed a British fort. New England loves its historic eminence. As you enter a New England town, welcome signs include the year of incorporation, as though they're in competition.

Another struggle for superiority among New England towns involved where and when the Revolutionary War began. Prelude to Revolution: The Salem Gunpowder Raid of 1775 by Peter Hoffer, published in 2013, contends it started in Salem. On February 26, 1775, residents thwarted a plan by British soldiers to take the colonists' gunpowder.

The colonists raised North Bridge to keep British soldiers away from their gunpowder. The British commander, Colonel Leslie, had orders to cross the bridge. A local pastor allowed the colonel to cross the drawbridge if he agreed to go back over the bridge immediately. The colonel agreed and fulfilled his orders. The actions of the colonists stopped the British in Salem, but it wasn't a battle.

Winter Island Boat Yard resides along the causeway connecting Winter Island to downtown Salem. An eight-foot fence concealed the apparatus inside; boat lifts, boat stands, tools, arched boat sheds, and, of course, boats tucked any place they'd fit. Tim pulled the car alongside the house/office. Across the yard, a dark blue, thirty-one-foot Ranger Tug appeared suspended in the air. It rested on stanchions with a large ladder at the stern.

Juniper Cove, next to the boatyard, drained by low tide, exposed a broad expanse of mudflats. Boats leaned on the muck, hulls laid bare. They looked like toys strewn across a child's floor. Grounded, the boats waited for Massachusetts Bay's tide to fill the cove and resurrect them. Across the cove, fine old houses with widow's walks conjured images of ladies in long dresses staring out at the sea, waiting for their men to return.

We climbed the outside staircase to the office, and Tim introduced himself. Peter, the owner of the yard, expected us. Tall and trim, with sun-bleached hair, he wore workman's clothes and Top-Siders. Peter gave us a little background as he led the way across the boatyard.

"The owner lives in Falmouth, Massachusetts, and worked for the Sox," Peter told us. "That's why it's called *Extra Innings*."

"That's funny," I said. "Tim's a Yankees fan, and we live in Falmouth, Maine."

We boarded the boat via the ladder at the stern and looked around as Peter told us about the features and maintenance history. Inside the door on the left were two electrical panels, one for AC and the other for DC. A reckoning took place as I stared at the two panels. This boat's operation required a sharp learning curve. I ignored the cautious voice in my head that warned: This is a bad idea. Instead, I listened to the confident, excited voice saying what a grand adventure this would be.

We gave *Extra Innings* a thorough examination and thanked Peter. In town, we lunched at the Witch's Brew Café and discussed our plans. It was a big decision. As we sat down at our table, Tim asked, "What did you think?"

"I really liked it. There seemed to be a good amount of room and nice outside space."

"It looked like it was in excellent condition," Tim replied.

I trusted Tim to be the responsible party. We finished our lunch and walked down Derby Street. Shops and restaurants lined the route, some with mystical paraphernalia, others with witch-themed tourist tchotchkes, and still others imitated the original merchants' stores.

Beyond the boat itself, an unspoken detail hovered in the air. Purchasing the boat in Massachusetts meant we would be returning to Florida via the North Atlantic Ocean and the Intracoastal Waterway.

We had spoken about long-distance cruising and taking the ICW down the coast, but that was hypothetical. Regardless, it seemed premature to worry about piloting it to Florida when we hadn't made an offer.

"If we're going to do this, we need to have the two surveys done," Tim said.

"Surveys?"

"Yeah, a marine surveyor will check everything out while it's on land, and then you have a sea trial to test it in the water."

"That makes sense."

"So, we have to be pretty serious if we're paying for the surveys."

We strolled by the Salem Custom House, then down Derby Wharf, and continued our discussions. Tied up at the dock, a three-masted vessel named Friendship of Salem reminded visitors of Salem's seafaring history. The original vessel, built in 1796, brought goods to Salem from all over the world. The replica before us, built in 1996, fueled my desire to have a taste of that life for myself.

We made an offer. If we could agree on a price, we'd move forward. The owner had two previous offers that had fallen through. We hoped that would benefit us. After negotiating a price, everything needed to be tested, on land and on the water. I was being tested too. Traveling 1,500 miles by boat scared the hell out of me.

When I bought the little house in Hampton Falls, I had opened the door to a new life. I learned the pursuit of happiness began with showing up and sometimes being terrified. That lesson fortified my resolve to take on this adventure with Tim. I wanted nothing more than to grab hold of life and hang on for the ride, fear be damned.

As we drove back to Salem for the first survey of the boat, I gazed at the ring around my finger. It confirmed the odyssey of my life. My journey of self discovery and sadness brought me to this place. Before leaving Florida, we had mailed out "save the date" cards announcing our wedding plans, not knowing we'd be returning to Florida by boat. Now, a confluence of events approached—this journey, our wedding, and several art shows I had signed up for in Florida. It felt like a tidal wave gaining momentum offshore was about to swallow me. The time had arrived to hold my breath and push forward once again.

We arrived at Winter Island Boatyard where we met Scott, a burly Mainer with a heavy accent. Once again, we climbed the ladder at *Extra Innings'* stern. I listened carefully as he walked us through the function and condition of each system. If I were to be of any use on this journey, I'd do my best to learn the technical parts.

We told Scott about our plans to take the boat to Florida.

"She's perfect for a trip like that. You should have no trouble. I've made that trip a dozen times."

"That's reassuring," I said.

"It's a great trip," he continued. "I've brought down boats for folks who didn't feel comfortable making the trip themselves. Whether you take the ICW or you want to go a little faster on the outside, you'll be fine. Ranger Tugs are well-built, sturdy boats."

Two weeks later, the sea trial took place at 9:00 a.m. The day was gray, with a storm brewing. In addition to Peter, Tim, and me, there were several other participants. A yacht broker from Florida came for the sea trial, and Scott brought his assistant, Dave.

Peter led the way, effortlessly descending the rickety wooden ladder attached to the seawall. A well-used dinghy was tied up to the dock, eight feet below. The men all piled in. As they filed down the ladder, I waited for my turn, palms sweating. I always wanted to do what the boys did growing up. This was no different. I followed along, gingerly stepping on the weathered rungs and onto the dock. A deep breath of salty air filled my lungs as I braced myself for the ride in the scarred rubber craft.

Moored outside the narrow opening of Jupiter Cove, *Extra Innings* bobbed in the choppy waters. The dark blue hull stood out against the gray clouds hovering over Salem Sound. I stepped onto the swim platform in the stern and smiled at the thought of one day jumping off that platform into the warm Florida waters.

On board, further discussions of the boat's features and operation began. Tim paid close attention to the discussion about the helm. When they started with the electrical panels, it was my turn to listen up.

As the inspection progressed and the men saw my interest, they addressed the explanations to me as well as Tim. Our team approach felt good. Learning as much as possible was key to being a full partner. I would never know boating as well as Tim, but understanding the systems gave me purpose.

Peter turned on the ignition, and we started out. At Scott's request, Peter moved the throttle forward, pushing the engine harder. Scott explained how the boat could plane above the choppy water at higher speeds.

Peter invited Tim to take the wheel. The GPS screen in front of him mapped our course. Beyond the navigational systems, there were more functions to check: the heater, the generator, the air conditioner, and more. Seeing all the comforts the boat provided encouraged my hesitant self, but learning the systems intimidated me.

We pulled up to the town dock as the inspection continued. Scott

Sea trial

pushed a button to lift the engine cover. A diesel engine filled the compartment, along with a labyrinth of cylinders, hoses, and valves. On deck, I listened as Scott went over the systems while testing them.

"You won't need this on now," Peter said as he turned a ball valve to its closed position. "This is for the heat." Remembering that little snippet of conversation a few weeks later would secure my position as chief engineer.

It was a remarkable thing to watch Peter maneuver his long, trim body into the engine compartment. The air conditioning wasn't working. He reached over, opened a small door under the bench, and pulled out a hose.

"I'm going to prime the pump. This hose pulls in seawater," he said as he removed the top of a clear plastic cylinder.

"Dave, turn on the hose." Dave went to the DC panel and flipped a switch.

"This will get it going," he said as he sprayed water into the cylinder.

"What's the one next to it for?" I asked.

There was another cylinder that looked identical.

"That's for cooling the engine," Peter responded.

Scott and Dave finished the inspection, and we stepped onto the dock, admiring the boat. There was so much to learn. I wondered if I'd ever be able to remember it all. Scott issued the report a week later.

CHAPTER 21

LITTLE PRINCE

And now here is my secret, a very simple secret:
it is only with the heart that one can see rightly,
what is essential is invisible to the eye.
—Antoine de Saint-Exupéry, *The Little Prince*

It passed the inspection, but some minor work needed to be done, and the owner agreed to split the cost. To complete the registration, the boat needed a name. Tim wanted nothing silly in case we needed to call the Coast Guard. I Googled names, but nothing jumped out at me.

I read the myths and lore of boat names with curiosity. I didn't want to tempt fate or succumb to foolishness. One legend warned not to be too audacious in naming your boat because it angers Poseidon. Oddly, that seemed reasonable.

Apparently, it's bad luck to rename a boat without performing a ritual. Before the ritual can take place, all traces of the previous name must be removed from the boat. We needed two bottles of champagne, a metal tag with the old name written on it, and incantations to Poseidon to perform the ritual. "The Ledger of the Deep" is Poseidon's list of boats on the ocean. He protects the boats on the ledger. If we didn't perform the ritual, our boat name wouldn't be on the list, and we wouldn't be afforded Poseidon's protection.

Time and common sense prevented the ritual. I hoped removing all traces of the old name sufficed. I left a package of napkins with baseballs on them in one drawer. While they didn't have *Extra Innings* printed on them, I wondered if keeping them was a mistake. Did they count?

I wanted our boat name to have meaning. Tim suggested the Intrepid Artist, after me, but we weren't sure. One morning, I awoke before the sun came up, unable to get back to sleep. Boat names raced through my head. I went downstairs, curled up on the couch with a throw, and started searching online for my favorite books. Maybe something from literature would work.

It wasn't long before I came across *The Little Prince* by Antoine de Saint-Exupéry. My memory failed me. I knew I loved the book, but I couldn't remember the story. I found it online and settled into reading.

The inspiration I sought unfolded with each chapter and each planet the Little Prince visited. From his travels, the Little Prince learned love is the thread that binds all things. Too often, when people become adults, they're caught up in things that aren't important, like counting things and being in charge. We should hold on to the curiosity and wonderment children possess to experience life more fully.

Soft light gradually illuminated the room as day broke. I looked out the front windows. The sun was just over the horizon. A ribbon of orange bounced on the surface of Casco Bay. I smiled, remembering the first time I'd visited Tim's house and looked out at the bay. It seemed like a lifetime ago. I turned the page and continued reading, but I knew the name fit. Tim agreed.

Little Prince, it would be.

Time seemed to get away from us with all there was to do. Would the inflatable dinghy be sufficient for this trip? After some research, we found a dinghy made in Portland, Maine, called a "Portland Pudgy." The design made it almost impossible to tip over. Given my trepidation with dinghies, I jumped at the suggestion of buying it.

As the day to take possession of *Little Prince* neared, I assumed my role as navigator/first mate. I mapped out the course from Salem, Massachusetts, to Falmouth, Maine, for practice. The chart plotter on board provided our primary navigational tool, but a paper backup ensured a safe trip. I had watched Tim chart a course on previous occasions, and the boating courses I'd taken covered some of it, so I thought I'd give it a try.

The first step was to find the right chart and find Winter Island. What to do beyond that became a ball of confusion. The land was colored yellow, shallow water was blue, and deeper water, white. Numbers displaying water depths crawled all over the paper like tiny ants. All kinds of lines ran across it, starting with latitude and longitude, which formed a grid on the page. I vaguely remembered those from geography class, circa 1972. Back then, I had thought it was like quadratic equations, a part of that vast array of information I'd never use. I remembered latitude was east-west. "Think of rungs on a ladder," the teacher had said.

Distinct lines with numbers attached to them crisscrossed the chart in a haphazard way. Those lines listed the distance between navigational markers: buoys, bells, and nuns in nautical miles and direction written in degrees (another one of those long-forgotten geography tidbits). My favorite notations were the warnings about unexploded ordnance, unexploded mines, or even the occasional unexploded depth charge.

The last week in August we got the call; *Little Prince* was ready. Excited but nervous, I helped pack the car with supplies we'd need to pilot the boat to Maine and a cooler with our lunch. The weather cooperated for our hundred-mile maiden voyage, with sunny skies and temperatures in the eighties.

Peter greeted us in the office. He reviewed the completed work, but there was an issue. The end of the oil dipstick for the generator was broken off. He couldn't say if there was sufficient oil in the generator. The new dipstick would be shipped to us in Maine. In the meantime, he cautioned us not to use the generator. With that, we headed outside.

I saw *Little Prince* tied up along the same dock we had used to board the dinghy during the sea trial. How will we get our stuff on board climbing down that ladder?

"I'll move her to the other dock so you can put your things on board," he said.

I felt a sigh of relief as we walked to the car to get our knapsacks, charts, and cooler.

On board, Peter again went over the controls with us. Then we were on our own. Juniper Cove was mud flats the first time we went to Winter Island Boatyard. With that image in mind, I anxiously waited to get underway before the tide went out, while Tim calmly ate his lunch. At the same time, I struggled with processing all the information about the boat's systems. I desperately tried to keep my emotions in check, but fear of the unknown took its toll. After half a sandwich, my nerves clenched my stomach, and I urged Tim to finish eating.

Our destination for the night was Newburyport, Massachusetts. I had exhibited my paintings in several of the Newburyport Art Association shows. Hampton Falls was a twenty-minute drive from Newburyport. It's a great town with lots of restaurants, so returning there would be comforting.

Before we could get to Newburyport, we needed to deal with Cape Ann, home of the city of Gloucester and the town of Rockport. Cape Ann was first mapped by the explorer John Smith, of Jamestown Colony fame, and colonized in 1623. Captain Smith had shown his map to Charles I, King of England, who had named Cape Ann after his mother, Ann of Denmark.

Going around the cape, farther into the Atlantic, would add time and miles to our trip. The other option was to proceed up the Annisquam River, which separates Cape Ann from the mainland and connects with Ipswich Bay. We opted for the river as the more prudent route.

We entered Gloucester Harbor and looked for the drawbridge to the Annisquam River. Using binoculars, I saw the narrow entrance and a line of boats waiting. I pointed it out to Tim, and he headed in that direction.

As we waited for the bridge to open, a line of spectators formed along the fence on the street above. It seemed a rather curious development. With warning bells ringing and guardrails coming down across the road, the bascule bridge started rising, revealing a line of boats waiting to enter Gloucester Harbor. The boats on the other side had the right-of-way. Traveling with the current, they moved easily between the narrow concrete walls of the bridge, but they created a significant amount of wake.

Next, the harborside boats started moving. An alarming scene unfolded. The combination of wake from previous boats, the narrow opening, and traveling against the tide created a precarious situation. We watched the boats ahead of us surge forward and head toward the opposite wall of the bridge, then pivot right to enter the river. One after another, the bows of the boats rocketed skyward as they hit the wake. It became clear why spectators had lined up to watch. With only two hours of piloting *Little Prince*, Tim needed to replicate the dangerous maneuver. Eyes wide, Tim and I turned and looked at each other.

"Holy shit," Tim said.

We watched the smaller boat in front of *Little Prince* spring forward. The captain leaned over the wheel, gripping it with both hands; his passenger clutched the railing and a metal post supporting the canopy. Up went the bow as it plunged into the wake and crested the wall of water. With one quick motion, the captain turned the wheel to starboard, cleared the bridge, and avoided the river's rocky embankment.

"Hold on," Tim said.

I gripped the handrail in front of me, my heart pounding. With one hand on the wheel, the other on the throttle, Tim accelerated, hurling our bow toward the abutment and the oncoming wake, then turned the wheel to the right. The stony riverbank was no longer in front of us. Tim throttled down as we converged with the Annisquam River.

"Wow," I said, and let out a breath I didn't realize I'd been holding.

"We were lucky the guys in front of us had local knowledge," Tim said.

"What?"

"Local knowledge. It's when boaters have information about their waters. Things you won't find in waterway guides. Without seeing what the boats in front of us did, we may have hit the abutment."

"Yeah, 'cause if this was in the guide, I would have walked back to Maine."

"It wasn't that bad. Just relax, and enjoy the ride."

"I'm trying."

"Are you sure you want to go all the way to Florida by boat?"

"I'll be fine. It takes a little getting used to. You've had way more experience than me."

"Not with this boat."

We passed under another bridge connecting Cape Ann with the mainland. The tranquil setting along the river contrasted with Gloucester Harbor. Houses lined one side of the river; marshes, the other. Moored boats rested on the tidal estuary. Annisquam Harbor Lighthouse stood watch on Wigwam Point where the Annisquam River ended.

We traversed Ipswich Bay and continued around Plum Island before making our way up the Merrimack River to Newburyport. Tim negotiated a mooring for the night at the local yacht club. The mooring line was slimy and black from sitting in the water for ages, maybe since the last time Paul Revere had passed by. We radioed for the launch to take us ashore. The launch pilot informed us it would be running for only another hour.

With that tidbit, we decided on takeout and found a market that sold salads and sandwiches.

"Let's eat here and sit at the table outside," Tim said.

"I'm good with getting food here, but I just want to get back on *Little Prince*. I don't want to miss the launch."

"We have time."

"No. My nerves are shot. I've had enough for one day. I just want to relax."

CHAPTER 22

PREPARATIONS

There are far better things ahead than any we leave behind.
—C.S. Lewis

That evening in Newburyport, I didn't want to push my luck. Exhaustion consumed me after eight hours on *Little Prince*. Back on board, Tim ate his sandwich, and I nibbled at my pasta salad, still trying to settle my nerves. Tim opened a bottle of wine, and I began to relax. We watched the sun setting over the town. The church steeple soared above the rooftops, catching the pale orange glow of sunset. When darkness fell, a spotlight lit the spire.

Dusk invited the mosquitos to join us, invading our peaceful evening. We retreated into the cabin to escape and opened the windows. My window refused to open. The muggy night showed no mercy. The air hung still and heavy. Without the generator to run the air conditioning, we had few options. First, the shirts came off, then pants. Soon we were sipping wine in our underwear. On our first night on *Little Prince*, was this just comic relief or a harbinger of things to come?

The gentle motion of the tides rocked us to sleep. Dawn and the sound of boats passing woke us. The early sun twinkled like stars in the rippling water. Well rested, I stepped outside and inhaled deep, restorative breaths of cool morning air. We watched other boats zip by, each following the same route.

"It's low tide," Tim said.

"Are we okay?" I asked.

"Yeah, but we need to take the same route the other boats are taking."

"Local knowledge?"

"Yup. We'll be fine. I'll keep an eye on the depth to be sure. You want to get the mooring line? I'll fire up the engine."

We made our way to the mouth of the Merrimack River. Out on the ocean, deep water, calm seas, and familiar places eased my trepidation. We ventured up to the flybridge for a better view. On the navigation screen, I saw Seabrook and Hampton Beach. I looked for Hampton Beach's water tower or anything I could recognize. I wanted to see the church steeple in Hampton Falls around the corner from my old house. In the days before GPS technology, sailors used church steeples as an aid to navigation. Before I located the steeple, the Isles of Shoals emerged on the horizon.

I had always wanted to go there and see the islands but had never found the time. Six miles off the coast, some islands in the group are in Maine, and the rest are in New Hampshire. Four hundred years of history offered a variety of tales about life on the islands. In 1628, the Puritans of Massachusetts Bay Colony exiled Thomas Morton to one island for consorting with the native population.

Appledore and Star Islands are the largest of the archipelago. To avoid taxes during the colonial period, European settlers of Appledore Island in Maine fled to Star Island in New Hampshire. Celia Thaxter, a well known writer, welcomed notable artists to the Appledore House built in 1847. She hosted artists and writers, including Childe Hassam, William Morris Hunt, Ralph Waldo Emerson, and Henry Wadsworth Longfellow. Her father owned the hotel and manned the lighthouse.

Today, Shoals Marine Laboratory occupies Appledore Island. Cornell University and the University of New Hampshire maintain the educational facility on Appledore.

Up on the flybridge, I photographed the sparsely populated islands. They appeared mystical through the morning haze. Perched on the rocky shore, the "White Island Light" captured my attention first. A house on the cliffs of Star Island stood on stilts and rock with a moored lobster boat below the front deck. The rugged beauty of it all intrigued me.

Tim engaged the automatic pilot, and we sat up top like mere passengers enjoying the ride. The sunshine, salt air, and closeness to home made the last leg of our journey delightful. My nerves calmed. I looked forward to our trip down the ICW. After six hours on the water, we cruised by Cape Elizabeth and entered Casco Bay. Completion of our shakedown cruise brought a sense of relief and accomplishment. My confidence grew with each familiar sight. I pulled up the mooring line on our buoy and secured *Little Prince*. It was good to be home, but we had no time to relax.

By now, it was the middle of August. We had anticipated taking possession of the boat earlier in the summer. The later our launch date, the more ominous the weather factor. Cold temperatures, high winds, and rough seas would arrive soon, and we had a lot of preparations to make before we left.

White Island

Once home, Tim called his friend John, a local harbormaster and active member of America's Boating Club, to perform a safety inspection. He had a similar boat, so he might help us get better acquainted with the features of *Little Prince*. He was also the instructor of a boating class I'd taken, "Second in Command."

John arrived and went to work while I took notes. He pulled the life jackets out of the locker in the stern to count and inspect them. He then pulled out some metal objects.

"You have davits," he declared.

"We do?" Tim responded.

"Look," John said as he arranged the items in proper order.

"Wow, that's great," Tim said.

"You just saved a few hundred dollars," John said.

Davits are attached to the stern to secure the dinghy on the boat. John finished up with a list of replacement parts we should have as extras. In the end, we passed our safety inspection and gained a little more confidence in our plan.

The new dipstick arrived. After unsuccessfully trying to guide it into place, maneuvering around twists and turns, I looked at the manual. From the diagram, I knew which way to go and guided it into place. Quite pleased with myself, I tried to start the generator. Nothing, not a sound when I depressed the "on" switch in the cabin.

The routine maintenance check by Handy Boat, our boatyard, grew to include a look at the generator. For a moment, Tim considered attaching the davits himself but realized the task was above his pay grade and added it to Handy Boat's list. Roger, an experienced diesel mechanic, conducted the inspection. Once again, I took notes and drew diagrams. Roger ordered all the spare parts we should have on board. Everyone we spoke with had a different idea of the parts we needed. Having someone of Roger's expertise make a list and order the parts took the burden off us.

The problem with the generator stumped Stephanie, a technician at Handy Boat. Tim made an appointment for a technician from the manufacturer to come out and have a look. We brought *Little Prince* up to the dock to meet him. In a matter of minutes, he solved the problem. I unknowingly had tripped the on-off switch on the generator when I'd inserted the dipstick. We didn't even know the hidden switch existed. He asked if we had any other questions since we were already paying for the one hour service call. He gave us a thorough explanation of the generator's workings and how best to use it. More information to file in my already taxed brain.

We sat at the dock deciding what to do next when our neighbor Bob came by with a bottle of wine, wishing us a bon voyage. Bob had sailed down the East Coast in his sailboat several years back and made some recommendations. We showed him around the boat.

"This is a very seaworthy boat," he commented.

When Bob left, Tim fired up the engine for more practice at maneuvering and anchoring. Sailing *Respite* around the lobster pots can be tricky depending on the wind. Motoring around them gave us more experience in handling *Little Prince*. We headed toward Little Chebeague Island to practice anchoring.

Preparations and arrangements continued. I contacted a transport company to pick up the car and truck it to Florida. Tim called the plumber. He didn't want to pay to heat the house through the winter, which meant a plumber needed to drain the pipes so they wouldn't freeze and burst. Also, the electric company needed to shut off the power. Coordinating the timing of all the final arrangements became critical.

As I gathered nonperishable food, tools, and cooking implements Tim jokingly referred to me as "The Quartermaster," a term I'd heard but never understood, until then. The task of finding places on the boat for everything we'd need, given limited space and a trip that would take at least a month, challenged my meager organizational skills.

I focused on the galley first. The granite countertop gave the appearance of a modern kitchen. But the stove, a double-bowl sink, four drawers, and a cabinet below the sink all lined up were smaller than an average-sized kitchen table. A compact refrigerator resided under the counter next to the drawers. The most vital appliances were set into the foundation of the benches across the aisle—a miniature micro-wave oven and the wine fridge.

I read about cooking on a boat. Given the limited space, I considered all recommendations carefully. Nested pots, a wide-mouth thermos, and a couple of little hammocks for additional storage of fruits and vegetables seemed to be the most practical. My go-to place for outfitting the galley became a discount store with a vast array of plastic containers.

The midcabin berth known as "the cave" by Ranger Tug owners, would have to handle most of our storage needs. The space is concealed by a smoked glass door just inside the back of the main cabin on the port side. Two steps down lead to a mattress squeezed into a space four feet wide by three feet tall, narrowing at the far end. As sleeping quarters for a child, it's perfect, but not for adults—unless you don't like them very much. For our purposes, it housed tools, cushions for outside use, charts, and anything else that needed to be stowed on board.

Tim ordered six chart books, starting with the Canadian Border to Block Island, Rhode Island down to Florida's West Coast, one for each leg of our journey. In addition, he ordered four cruising guides that covered the same territory. The charts provided all the navigational data we needed. The cruising guides provided a wealth of information about marinas, bridge heights, places to purchase fuel, and visitor information.

The Portland Pudgy folks delivered the dinghy to Handy Boat. The boatyard hauled *Little Prince* out of the water to install the davits. With *Little Prince* perched on stanchions in the boatyard, or "on the hard," we buffed the hull. Our tentative launch date, September 22, drew closer.

At times, my lust for adventure exceeded my fortitude. This became one of those times. I retreated to the kitchen. As always, cooking calmed my nerves, and I needed to make food ahead of the trip that I could freeze and reheat easily on the boat. The process began with spaghetti sauce simmering on the stove. Its mouthwatering scent filled the cottage. A plate of newly formed meatballs waited for their turn in the frying pan, while the first batch sizzled and hissed. The sound of clattering pots and pans mingled with the music of Andrea Bocelli and Luciano Pavarotti. My sauce improved when I played Italian classics. The next day the savory aroma of meatloaf, beef stew, and chili filled the house. Time in the kitchen kept at bay the voice in my head that threatened to turn my excitement into panic. I cooked until the freezer was filled.

My last grand escapade had occurred five years earlier, and I went through the same roller coaster of emotions. When an opportunity to paint in the Rocky Mountains presented itself, I jumped at the chance. A solo drive to Colorado sounded liberating. Long-distance drives weren't foreign to me, but traveling alone brought a different perspective. I had planned to stay with family along the way. Panic struck on the day I started my trip.

After four hours of driving, I stopped in New Jersey for lunch with my brother Jim and his family. At lunch, I picked at my food, too

Little Prince, Barbara, and Tim

nervous to eat. Per my typical modus operandi, I loved the thought of some endeavor, but when the time to launch arrived, excitement turned to dread. More times than not, I found myself saying, "What the hell were you thinking?" This boat trip fell into the same pattern.

As our day for leaving approached, I called Jim for reassurance.

I started the conversation with, "Remember when I drove by myself out to Colorado and how nervous I got?"

"Oh, this is way worse than that," he shot back.

Note to self: When looking for a "you got this," don't call your brother.

CHAPTER 23

AND SO IT BEGINS

You can. You should.
And if you are brave enough to start, you will.
—Stephen King

Tim set a date with the plumber to drain the pipes in the house. Twice the plumber called to reschedule; emergency calls took precedence. We took clothes, charts, and nonperishable provisions out to *Little Prince* while waiting for our appointment with the plumber. At the same time, the Coast Guard posted a small craft advisory. Hurricane Leslie churned up the Atlantic Ocean and created high seas. Even though we weren't ready to leave, the message was clear: the weather controlled our fate.

With every delay, the amount of daylight decreased, and the wind increased. Wind-generated waves. The harder the wind blew, the higher the waves rose.

Eventually, the stars aligned, and we had our day. The plumber came and began his work. There were complications. With a house that's more than a hundred years old, there were always complications. He would need to come back the next day to finish. Tim's cousin Judith and her husband, Greg, volunteered to deal with the plumber and invited us to spend the night at their house, across the street. After a lobster dinner at the Dockside Grill, we settled in for the night. I tried to calm my racing thoughts as I lay in bed staring at the ceiling. What might go wrong?

October 10 arrived with clear skies and temperatures expected to reach the high seventies. I pushed my panic down so far that only calm resolve remained. Tim was calm without misgivings.

We gathered things together, including Tigger's knapsack filled with his leash, bowls, and food. Any time I picked up his knapsack, Tigger sprang to attention, tail wagging. He stared at his bag as if to ask, "Where are we going?" The start of our expedition became Tigger's inaugural trip on *Little Prince*. I strapped on his personal flotation device (PFD) when we got to the yacht club. Poor Tigger had no idea what awaited him, nor did I.

As we walked to the dock, the earthy scent of exposed seagrass mingled with the salt air and hurled me into a sea of doubt. The wooden pier creaked under my feet. I passed through the dock house's steep-pitched roof and arched entry. At the top of the gangplank, I paused and gazed out at Falmouth Harbor: Ripples from the incoming tide plucked the sun's embers from the sky and sprinkled them over Casco Bay.

All the books I read and the boating classes I'd attended lured me into a fanciful semblance of confidence. Confronted with one hundred fifty nautical miles of open ocean in the North Atlantic, the glistening sunlight looked like broken glass. The anticipation of a subsequent seven hundred miles of bays and inland waterways strained my mettle. Uncertainty eclipsed my enthusiasm, but it was too late to alter our course, and I didn't want to.

I took a deep breath. My hand trembled as I reached for the cool metal handrail, knuckles white, second thoughts screamed in my head. In front of me, Tim guided a cart filled with last-minute supplies down the ramp. The jarring sound of metal clanking and rattling compelled me forward. I used the handrail to steady my descent while Tigger pulled on his leash.

Chuck stood by the launch and waited to take us out to *Little Prince*. He helped transfer our things from the cart. I held tight to Tigger's leash while Tim and Chuck chatted about our trip. Soon Anne, Tim's cousin, walked down the dock. She came to wish us a bon voyage and photograph the event.

We pulled away from the dock. Chuck headed toward *Little Prince*, moored at the far end of the anchorage, leaving behind the remaining boats. He maneuvered the launch alongside *Little Prince*. I boarded first, and Tim passed Tigger up to me, followed by some of the supplies. Tim climbed on board, and Chuck hoisted the cooler up to us. It was packed to the brim, and we hoped the meals I had prepared would sustain us for a week or more. I wrapped the food and a block of dry ice in a space blanket to keep everything frozen for as long as possible.

A mooring buoy from a neighbor's boat poked up behind the stern. It had become entangled with our rudder and propeller. We lowered the dinghy (Rose) into the water, keeping it securely attached to *Little Prince*. Tim stepped into the dinghy to assess the problem. He cut the tangled ancillary lines and left our neighbor's mooring line intact.

With all our other preparations, we had never tried to raise and lower Rose. When we grabbed the line to heave the dinghy back into place, Rose defied our efforts. The water acted like a suction cup, making the task more difficult than expected. We needed more lines, one line attached to the bow for Tim and one attached to Rose's stern for me. After a few tries, we learned to rock the dinghy and, on the count of three, wrench it out of the water and into place.

Tim started the engine and input waypoints into the navigation panel, and I cast off our mooring line. Tim eased the throttle forward. Fright surrendered to excitement. We're really doing this. We entered Portland Harbor and cruised by Portland Head Light and Ram Island Ledge Light, the same lighthouses Tim had brought me to the first time he'd taken me sailing.

The morning's nostalgic air continued when we passed Two Lights State Park on Cape Elizabeth. Tim had taken me to the park one autumn day, years ago. It overflowed with things I loved to paint—waves crashing on rocks, wildflowers, lighthouses. We walked the trail that winds along the coast. The deep blue ocean mirrored the brilliant sky, with the same vibrance we now experienced on day one of our journey.

I felt an intimate connection with that coastline. I had painted it after our visit. When I closed my gallery, a contract for display ads remained in force, with three more months remaining. Eric, the magazine publisher, loved the painting. He recognized it as the place where he had proposed to his wife. Instead of having to shell out money for ads that would never run, Eric agreed to take the painting in exchange.

"It should have worked," Eric said when I told him I was closing the gallery.

His words relieved me of feeling like a foolish dreamer. Sometimes paintings find the place where they belong. That painting belonged to Eric. Even if the gallery hadn't been a booming financial success, I accomplished something to be proud of. As we rounded Cape Elizabeth, the fond memory put a wistful smile on my face.

Five hours later, we caught sight of Whaleback Lighthouse and Portsmouth Harbor Lighthouse. More memories flooded my thoughts when I saw them. One morning, not long after I had opened the gallery, I drove to New Castle Beach at sunrise to take photos. I vacillated between the two lighthouses, both visible from my vantage point. Whaleback Light, granite and rugged, Portsmouth Harbor Light, white and pretty, each possessed its own charm. I painted a picture of Portsmouth Harbor Lighthouse and used the photos I took to teach a watercolor class.

Whaleback Lighthouse stands on an elevated ledge attached to Gerrish Island, Maine. High tide submerged the ledge connecting the lighthouse to the island. The earliest record of a ship crashing on Whaleback Ledge dates from 1733. The first lighthouse on the site, erected in 1830, had to be torn down because of storms and poor construction. One storm rattled the lighthouse so much it caused rocks in the walls to tumble to the floors. Over the years, the ledge destroyed unwary ships, even after the lighthouses were erected. A new tower went into service in 1872.

Portsmouth Harbor Lighthouse stands on a finger of land in the town of New Castle, New Hampshire, an island adjacent to Portsmouth. The British built a fort there in 1631, and in 1771, the first lighthouse. Originally called the Castle, it took on a new identity when the British renamed it Fort William and Mary, after the king and queen of England.

In 1774, Paul Revere rode to New Castle from Boston to warn residents that the British were advancing. That turned out not to be the case, but the news motivated the townspeople to charge the fort and seize the gunpowder against little British opposition. That gunpowder supplied the colonists in the Battle of Bunker Hill.

We pulled into Portsmouth Harbor and the Portsmouth Yacht Club dock, just after six o'clock. Portsmouth Harbor is at the mouth of the Piscataqua River and forms the border between New Hampshire and Maine. Tim settled up with the dockmaster while I walked Tigger. Getting Tigger to land became a recurring theme. I purchased a Piddle Place, with fake grass and a plastic fire hydrant, for use on the boat. Tigger would have none of it. As planned, we spent the night moored in the harbor.

Five years earlier, I had walked down Congress Street in Portsmouth to meet Tim for the first time. Five years of changes blended with a sense of déjà vu. It felt good to be in familiar territory. Downtown Portsmouth transported me back in time whenever I visited. Brick buildings lined the downtown. The gleaming white steeple of North Church pierced the sky and demanded attention. When I looked up at the connected buildings along Ceres Street, I thought of Mary Poppins and expected to see chimney sweeps dancing on the rooftops. Along the waterfront, a row of restaurants looked out to Old Harbor. We didn't go downtown on this trip, but it was close by.

Our first day drew to a close. I pulled the frozen stew from the cooler to heat it. The noise of the generator interrupted the quiet evening. The generator powered the microwave to heat our dinner. The air cooled as the sun set, perfect for sleeping.

When morning came, gray and foggy skies lingered. Tim turned on the weather radio. The Coast Guard had issued a small craft advisory for the day. The shelter of Portsmouth Harbor deluded me into believing only a thin layer of fog had caused the advisory.

"What do you want to do?" Tim asked.

"How bad could it be? It's just gray. It'll clear, don't you think?"

"It's up to you if you want to try it," Tim said.

"Let's. We've had so many delays. I wanna get moving."

"Okay, if you're up for it."

First, we motored to the dock to walk Tigger. I moved to the back of the boat, ready to hand Tim the stern line. As he exited the side door to tie up the bow, he bumped into the throttle. *Little Prince* went into reverse. We were set on a collision course with an impeccably restored classic Herreshoff sailboat docked to our stern.

"Tim!" I yelled.

He saw the boat backing itself up, jumped back in, threw it into neutral, and avoided contact with the Herreshoff, averting disaster.

A nice Tigger walk calmed my nerves. I always tried to give Tigger plenty of time outside because it would be hours before another walk was possible. A little beach onshore gave him room to run and get some exercise. With that chore completed, we headed back to the dock.

Tim and I stood on the dock next to *Little Prince*, ready to pick Tigger up and pass him to whoever boarded the boat first. Tigger had other ideas. Without warning, he hurled himself forward. His little legs reached for the side of the boat. He had grossly miscalculated. As though in slow motion, he tried to grab the side of the boat with his paws, but he couldn't hold on. The little dog slid down the hull and plunged into the cold water.

NAVIGATIONAL CHARTS*

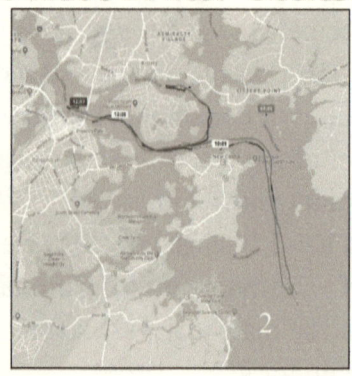

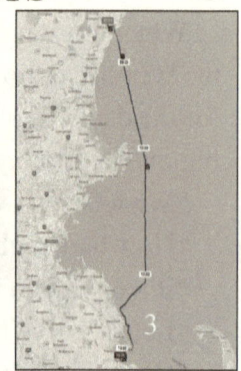

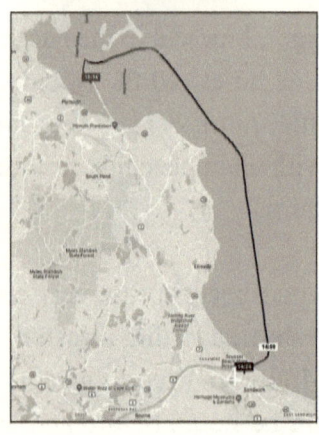

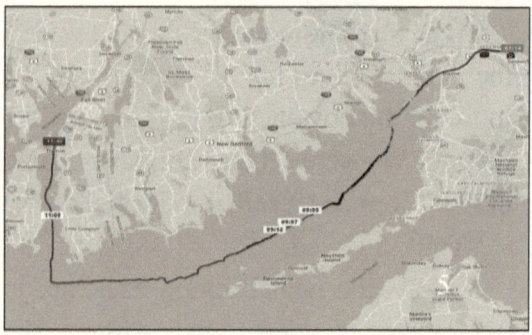

1.) Falmouth, Maine to
Portsmouth, N. H.

2.) Aborted due to rough seas

3.) Portsmouth to
Plymouth MA.

4.) Plymouth to Sandwich, MA.

5.) Sandwich to
Tiverton, R. I.

6.) Tiverton to Mystic, CT.

7.) Mystic to Branford, CT

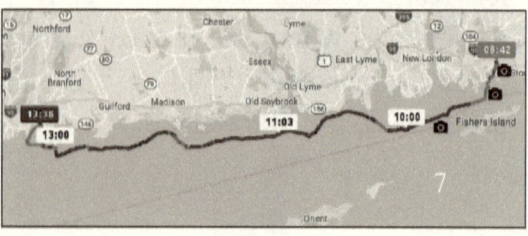

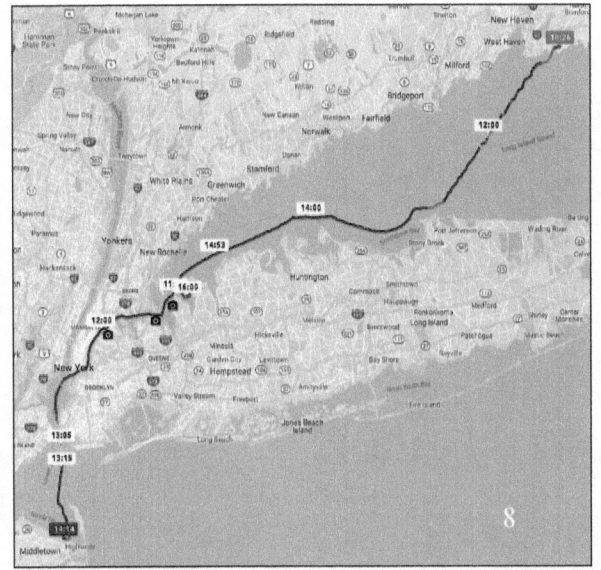

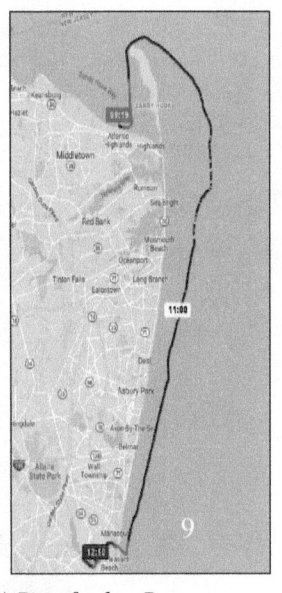

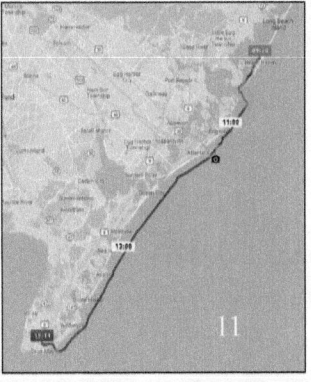

8.) Branford to Port Washington, N. Y. to Atlantic Highlands, N. J.

9.) Atlantic Highlands, to Manasquan, N.J.

10.) Manasquan to Long Beach Island, N.J.

11.) Long Beach Island to Cape May, N.J.

12.) Cape May to Georgetown, MD.

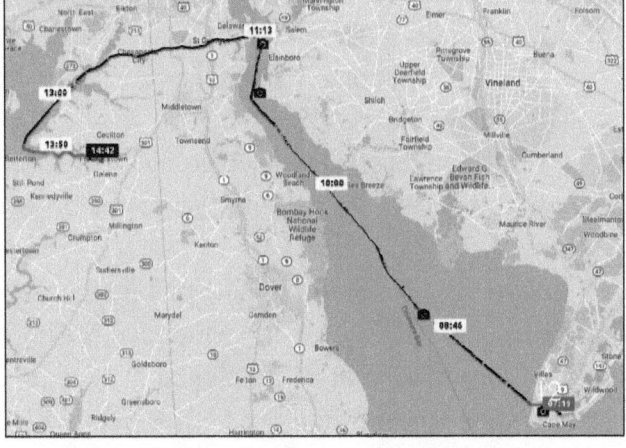

*Note: To see larger images in color go to https:// barbarabusenbark. com/charts/

Chapter 24

Safe Harbor

It is extraordinary to see the sea; what a spectacle!
She is so unfettered that one wonders
whether it is possible that she again become calm.
—Claude Monet

I jerked on Tigger's leash and landed his drenched, shivering body on the dock next to me. We got on board and quickly wrapped him in a towel and dried him off.

The bad omens continued. The small craft advisory waited for us outside the harbor. After all the delays, I longed to keep moving. I thought the fog would burn off and the calm water in the harbor meant acceptable conditions outside.

"Are you sure you want to keep going?" Tim asked a second time.

"Yeah. I wanna at least feel like we've made some progress."

"If you say so."

We passed by Portsmouth Harbor Lighthouse, then Whaleback Lighthouse. The swells grew as we rounded Jaffrey Point. By the time we passed Odiorne Point, I questioned my judgment. Safety should have been the highest priority, yet I was being driven by impatience. The foreboding clouds ahead and the pitching of *Little Prince* up and through the whitecaps scared me. A chorus of comments ("Ranger Tugs are well-built boats" and "This is a seaworthy boat") echoed in my head.

When we reached the open water of the Atlantic Ocean, the waves continued to mount in height and frequency. The farther we went, the worse it got. Tim steered *Little Prince*'s bow into the waves. Their force propelled the bow upward, only to be plunged into the trough of the wave with a pounding thud. It was a roller-coaster ride with Mother Nature at the controls. Six-foot waves came in rapid succession. I grabbed onto the safety bar in front of me.

Everything on the galley table and counter tumbled to the floor. Tigger took cover from the falling objects, leaning into the base of my seat. The combined sounds of swirling wind, pounding boat hull, and falling galley items increased my anxiety.

Water splashed over the windshield as the boat heaved up from the trough to plow through the next wave and plummet down again. A perverse rhythm dominated our ride. I was certain *Little Prince* wouldn't break apart with each impact. But doubts lingered. The spray interrupted the mass of gray sky and water that surrounded us. The rain and fog limited our visibility to one mile. Thirty-knot wind gusts further angered the sea. I flashed back to the boating course we had taken in Florida. Coast Guard officer Phil recounted his worst day at sea in the North Atlantic. The waves threw him out of his bunk, up and over a safety bar. The conditions he'd experienced surpassed ours, but comparing *Little Prince* to a Coast Guard cutter is like calling the family car a tank.

"Do you want to keep going?" Tim asked.

"No!"

Tim turned around and headed back to the safety of the harbor— lesson learned.

We returned to Portsmouth Harbor. The dramatic difference in conditions made clear what "safe harbor" meant. We found a slip available at Badger Island Marina, on the other side of Memorial Bridge. Tim radioed the bridge tender for an opening.

This became our first experience using shore power. We asked George, the dockmaster if someone could help us hook up. He gave us Darren's phone number. Sorting out what systems work with which power source presented a challenge.

There were two electrical panels, AC and DC. The AC uses shore power, and the DC uses the batteries. Then there are the inverter and the generator. Understanding how they were all interconnected got complicated. Tim called the phone number, and Darren came to the rescue. On arrival, we learned Darren owned the marina. Not only did he help us with the outlets, the stove, and the microwave, but he also showed us the proper way to run our cords to the power post on the dock. We shut everything off on the panels before plugging the two power cables into the power source. Next, I turned the knob to shore power and flipped on the switches of items as needed.

I asked Darren about the configuration of unrelated functions bundled together. "You'd have to ask the guys who engineered this boat. Sometimes they do crazy things, but they have their reasons," he responded. Darren complimented me on my interest, followed by, "I can't get my wife on a boat for anything." The man owned a marina and had a wife who wouldn't get on a boat.

Feeling comfortable and confident at day's end, I rummaged around in the cooler for dinner. Frozen vegetables acted both as an ice pack in the cooler and as a side dish. The gray day turned into a gray evening and called for comfort food—meatloaf.

Day two ended with one remaining glitch. Once it got dark, we realized the bathroom light no longer worked, a baffling issue. A small flashlight for nighttime use solved the problem.

The temperature plummeted. Days two and three reached a high of fifty-five and dropped to forty-five at night. We turned the heat on, but the blowing air remained cold. When I cooked the meatloaf in the oven, it warmed the cabin. The next day, I struggled to remember how to turn on the heat. Then it came to me. When we took part in the sea trial in July, Peter had reached into the engine compartment, turned a lever, and said, "You won't need the heat on now."

I reminded Tim and opened the engine compartment. I located the lever in the vicinity Peter had been in and turned it over. Tim turned on the heat and felt the warm air come from the vent. Success, but we were still in Maine.

The time in Portsmouth Harbor gave us the opportunity to get more comfortable with the boat's interior. Our stateroom in the bow, two steps down from the main cabin, contained an odd-shaped bed and the head. Absent the cutout at the bottom corner of the bed, it might have been full-sized. We stored extra blankets and an electric mattress cover in the storage area under the bed. A cabinet with shelves for clothes also housed the circuit breakers. Every space seemed to have a dual purpose. I hung the second hammock above the head of the bed for T-shirts. A touch of romance included a string of lights surrounding the base of the bed. An additional set of speakers for playing music via Bluetooth and a TV completed the cozy cabin.

Day three brought another small craft advisory. I had learned my lesson. We planned to enjoy our stay on Badger Island with nearby shops and restaurants.

The commerce on the river entertained me. The bridge tender raised and lowered Memorial Bridge, a vertical lift bridge, multiple times during the day. All manner of ships passed through, including barges, fishing trawlers, and pleasure boats.

There are several types of drawbridges. Some open only at designated times, while others open when called on the radio. The boat captain calls the bridge tender and identifies his boat's name and whether it's a power boat or a sailboat. The bridge tender logs all boats calling for an opening. Boats have the right-of-way over the cars traversing the bridge because they were once the primary mode of transporting goods. While cargo ships are still a major factor in commerce, pleasure boats reap the benefit of being able to get bridge openings on call a good deal of the time.

For lunch, we walked over to Warren's Lobster House, less than a half mile up the road in Kittery, Maine. The lobster house opened in 1940 as a lobster shack with six stools. Now it's a 350-seat restaurant with a bakery and gift shop. It sits on the water on pilings and boasts the seacoast's finest salad bar. An extra day in Maine meant another day to eat lobster, and what better place than Warren's?

I had to try the clam chowder. I order chowder wherever I go, especially places claiming to be superior. Growing up in New Jersey, I liked both Manhattan style and New England clam chowder. As a child on vacation on Long Beach Island, my favorite chowder came from Morrison's Seafood. Closer to Manhattan style but with a clearer broth, it contained more vegetables than most chowders I'd tried. The mention of Manhattan clam chowder in New England causes an onslaught of emotionally charged refusals to admit it's a chowder at all. Warren's lobster and clam chowder won first prize at the prestigious Portsmouth Chowder Fest, and it made it into my top five.

By the time we returned to *Little Prince*, the sky had cleared. A commercial lobstering business nearby presented the perfect subject for a painting. The opportunity arrived to begin work on a watercolor journal of our travels. The working boats exuded character and displayed an array of colorful lobster buoys and round boat fenders.

While I busied myself with painting, Tim checked in with Mike Rizzo, a retired airline pilot who also had a Ranger Tug. Tim and Mike became acquainted when Tim asked a question on an online forum for Ranger Tugs. Mike and his wife had planned to cruise from Rhode Island to their house on the west coast of Florida. Mike knew a great deal about Ranger Tugs and tracking weather. He recommended weather apps and became Tim's go-to guy.

The clearing skies that evening looked promising as day three ended. We awoke to a gray morning, raining and forty-five degrees, but the coast guard lifted the small craft warning. Finally, we were underway again at 7:30 a.m. Tim radioed the bridge tender for an opening. The mouth of the Piscataqua and the Atlantic Ocean lay ahead. Once again, we passed the Portsmouth Lighthouse, beaming its light through the morning haze, then Whaleback Lighthouse. It felt like we were saying goodbye to an old friend. I hated leaving New Hampshire. The confluence of memories of loved ones, the way of life, and the beauty of the place always collided with the reality that I no longer lived there. Manageable waves rose before us when we left the safety of the harbor.

Our destination for the day was Sandwich, Massachusetts, on Cape Cod. Our trip from Falmouth to Portsmouth had totaled sixty-seven nautical miles and taken six hours. Portsmouth to Sandwich was fifty-five nautical miles. This time, we rounded Cape Ann instead of the slower route up the Annisquam River. We also avoided the traffic of Boston Harbor by traveling farther out to sea. Commercial vessels go in and out of the harbor twenty-four hours a day. The number of marinas in the area for pleasure craft ranges between fifty and sixty. We wanted to stay at a smaller venue.

A steady rain fell but didn't affect visibility. We hoped it would clear as the day wore on and the sun would work its way through the clouds. A mild wind came from the west. Two hours into our trip, the wind increased in intensity. The choppy water concerned us, but it was still early. We hoped conditions would improve. They didn't. After another couple of hours of increasing wind, the waves reached heights of six feet and continued to grow. By noon, we changed course. Tim navigated closer to shore to mitigate the deteriorating conditions.

It didn't help. A new onslaught of six-foot waves materialized. All four windshield wipers were engaged to maintain visibility. Each wave that washed over the bow doused the windshield the way a tractor-trailer on the highway splashes cars during a driving rain. The din of items tossed around the boat signaled it was time to find a safe harbor.

Chapter 25

Plymouth

The pilgrims on the Mayflower landed at Plymouth Rock. To my knowledge,
they didn't wait around for a return trip to Europe.
You settle some place with a purpose.
If you don't want to do that, stay home.
You avoid an awful lot of risks by not venturing outward.
—Buzz Aldrin

We had made progress. We were south of Boston Harbor. Tim thought there would be less fetch (wind that grows stronger over open water) if we moved closer to shore. Nothing he did helped. Fortunately, we weren't far from Plymouth, Massachusetts.

I looked through the cruising guide to see our options. The Plymouth Yacht Club, a marina, and the town's mooring field all looked promising. We traveled close to shore until we entered the harbor and the waves died down. Duxbury Pier Lighthouse greeted us, and I saw lighthouses in a whole new way. Instead of being pretty landmarks, they now represented safety. With the aid of the lighthouse and the channel markers, we worked our way to the marina.

The narrow channel snaked around Plymouth Beach and then the breakwater protecting the anchorage. It made me wonder how the

Mayflower had managed it, and then I learned about the shallop, a small boat stored in pieces in the hull. When they approached land, the ship's carpenter assembled the shallop for coastal exploration and to take people ashore. At first, the Pilgrims landed on Cape Cod but found it too sandy, unable to support crops. After further exploration in their shallop, they found Plymouth.

Tim radioed the marina for a slip. None were available, but the town's harbormaster had a mooring for us. We were safe for the night. The sun appeared and made the brisk forty-degree temperature tolerable.

Tigger's trip to shore became the highest priority after mooring *Little Prince*. That meant using Rose, the dinghy. We lowered it into

Tim reading the manual

the water, keeping it attached to *Little Prince* with the davits on the swim platform. Once in the water, Tim set up the outboard motor. He lifted it off its mount and onto Rose. He adjusted the controls, put it in neutral, and gave it a pull. Nothing. A few more tries netted the same result. Out came the manual. As the quartermaster, I retrieved it immediately. With Tim in the dinghy (still attached to *Little Prince*) I read the instructions aloud. The harbormaster came by.

"I see you with the motor and your wife with the manual, and I'm thinking this could get ugly. Let us know if you need a ride to shore." With that, he motored on.

"You need to put the kill switch in first," I told Tim.

"Does it say that?"

"Yes, and there's a diagram too."

"Let me see that," he said as he reached out for the manual.

"I can read, ya know," I said, handing over the manual.

He looked hard for another answer and, finding none, confessed, "The kill switch is on the mantel back at the house." It had been years since Tim had used an outboard motor. At that time, kill switches didn't exist. Today, no kill switch, no motor. Tim slid the oars into the oarlocks, and I put Tigger in his life jacket.

Introducing Tigger to Rose added an extra dimension to our travels. His PFD had a handle on it. I lifted him and passed him to Tim. There has never been a more agreeable dog than Tigger, so despite his apprehension with the whole adventure, he offered no resistance and cowered under Tim's feet as I climbed in. I tried my best to comfort Tigger as Tim rowed.

We tied up at the dinghy dock and had a nice, long walk around Fisherman's Memorial Park. We continued down Water Street to see Plymouth Rock. The exact significance of the rock in relation to the *Mayflower* landing is subject to some speculation, but it's a "must-see," however unimpressive it may be.

My New England friends were right. The rock, two feet in diameter, sat on sand ten feet below the sidewalk, fenced in like a ferocious tiger, with "1620" carved into it. An imposing monument, with more than a dozen columns, towered above the rock, reminiscent of a mausoleum for a king.

We hoped to see *Mayflower II*, a replica of the original, but it was in Mystic, Connecticut, for renovations. The original *Mayflower* didn't last long after Captain Christopher Jones, quarter owner of the *Mayflower*, returned to England with the ship. When Jones died in 1621, the other three owners wanted the ship appraised. In 1624, the High Court of Admiralty described the ship as "in ruins" and valued it at 128 pounds sterling.

The *Mayflower II*, built in the United Kingdom in 1955–56, celebrated the cooperation of the two countries during World War II and commemorated their friendship.

The temperature dropped with the setting sun—we returned to *Little Prince*. Before we called it a night, one more piece of business needed attention. The kill switch. Tim called his cousin Judith and asked her to get the kill switch off the mantel and ship it to my brother in New Jersey. We could get it from him when we arrived there. I then called Jim and explained our situation. It seemed like a good plan.

We needed to snuggle under a heavy blanket, declared it a one-dog night, and invited Tigger to join us in bed. In the morning, we bundled up to explore Plymouth. The previous night's chill lingered, reminding us we were still in New England.

We walked down Water Street in search of breakfast and found a lovely café. Tigger wasn't allowed inside, so we bought takeout and sat on a bench in Brewster Gardens to have our meal. Bright yellow mums lined the brick walkway. The lovely park occupied the corner of Water and Leyden streets, the plot of land granted to Elder William Brewster, a distinguished leader of the Pilgrims.

"Let's sit in Grandpa's Park," I said to Tim.

"My mother never told a lie in her life," he replied, "so there must be some truth to being descendants of William Brewster. But I couldn't tell you how."

"That's very cool. I'm just a mutt. My grandparents and

Burial Hill Cemetery

great-grandparents all came from different places. My grandmother told me we used to own the land Macy's was built on."

"Really? In New York?"

"Yeah, but when I asked my father, he said it was probably a cemetery, and we had someone buried there. My grandmother was prone to . . . embellishment."

After breakfast, we headed up the hill on Leyden Street, the oldest continuously occupied street in the United States, built by the Pilgrims in 1620. Originally called First Street, then Great Street, then Broad Street, in 1823 it was renamed Leyden Street after a city in the Netherlands to which the Pilgrims had first fled.

There were 102 people on board the *Mayflower*. After several delays, the ship set sail on September 6. The late start increased the risk of rough seas. With our own late start, I felt an odd kinship with the Pilgrims. It took them more than nine weeks to reach land. After just under a week on *Little Prince*, I wondered what must have been going through their heads. We had a home to get to. They didn't know what lay ahead.

Two steeples punctuated the top of the hill, the First Parish Church of Plymouth and the Church of the Pilgrimage. Both churches trace their roots back to the Pilgrims. They straddle the walkway into Burial Hill Cemetery. Many of the Pilgrims and early settlers of Plymouth Colony were buried there. Although the whereabouts of William Brewster's actual burial place are unknown, he's said to be there too.

Massive oak and maple trees cast shadows throughout the cemetery. Through the leaves, dappled light sprinkled the aged gravestones. The crisp, refreshing smell of autumn's arrival filled the air. The bright, open space of Plymouth Harbor below illuminated the scene with a mystical glow. Old names like "Phineas" and "Rebecca," etched in the granite stones, touched the past. The harsh New England weather wore away some inscriptions, evoking thoughts of their first winter. Walking among the old graves, my mind wandered.

After seeing William Brewster's name all over Plymouth, I became obsessed with the need to know more about Tim's connection and Plymouth's history. What I remembered of ninth-grade history didn't cover enough about the *Mayflower* and her passengers.

Months later and after hours of research, I found Tim's connection. William Brewster is Tim's ninth great-grandfather. The history of Plymouth Colony became personal. I read more about the history and early New England life. On the next trip to New England, I wanted to go back to see the refurbished ship and more historic sites.

Tim's family history differed from mine. Years earlier, I had investigated my maternal grandmother's genealogy as a present for Aunt Mary's ninetieth birthday. My mother, her sisters, and her brother knew very little of their own mother's past because she had died at age fifty. Aunt Mary loved her gift of information about Margaret, her mother. It taught me about the troubles immigrants had endured.

My grandmother's childhood reflected the harshness of life for immigrant families at the turn of the twentieth century. According to the census of 1900, Margaret was three years old, and her mother, Susanne Vienot Reynolds, was in the Philadelphia Almshouse and Hospital, a city hospital for the poor. Susanne died in the hospital at age thirty-five. She had emigrated from France thirteen years earlier. From the 1910 census, at age thirteen, Margaret worked as a maid and no longer attended school, having completed only the eighth grade.

Tim's family arrived on the *Mayflower*, but mine came on later ships, like *France, Caledonia,* and *La Bourgogne* sailing from Ireland, Italy, and France. Ellis Island logged the records of sixty-five million immigrants. Among those passengers were my grandparents and great-grandparents. Somehow, four hundred years after the landing of the *Mayflower*, Tim and I walked together along the same shoreline as the Pilgrims.

There are several famous descendants of the fifty-two survivors of the *Mayflower*. John Howland, an indentured servant, had an impressive list of heirs: Franklin Delano Roosevelt, George H. W. Bush, and George W. Bush. It wasn't just that Howland had made it through that first winter, but he had survived the trip.

For their own safety, the passengers on the *Mayflower* were kept in the tween deck, located above the cargo hold and below the upper deck. Three weeks into their journey, conditions on board deteriorated. Storms raged, forcing the sailors to lower the sails, preventing them from being torn apart and eliminating some of the stress on the ship's mast and hull.

In the shelter of the tween deck, John Howland was unaware of the fierce storm and turbulent conditions. Howland longed to go up on deck for some air. He reached the top of the stairs, stepped outside, and took a deep breath. The tumultuous water roared and hurled a savage wave at the *Mayflower*. The ship careened to one side and threw Howland overboard. In an act of desperation, and in one sweeping motion, he grabbed hold of a loose line hanging from the stern. He plunged into the frigid North Atlantic, still holding tight to the rope. Miraculously, a sailor saw the incident, seized the line, and hoisted Howland back on board, saving his life.

After our breakfast in Brewster Gardens and a walk around Burial Hill, we needed to continue our journey. Back on *Little Prince*, I released the mooring line, picked up Tigger, put him on the bench next to me, and off we went. Next stop, Sandwich, Massachusetts, on Cape Cod. Each time we headed out into open water, I took a deep breath and braced myself.

Tim switched on the radio for a marine forecast. Sunny, fifty-five degrees, winds one knot south, southeast. Tomorrow morning, sunny, winds seven to ten knots increasing to gale-force winds by afternoon, ranging from thirty-four to forty knots. I turned to look at Tim.

CHAPTER 26

BUZZARDS BAY

There's no point in worrying. It's always the things
you don't expect that get you.
—Grandpa Mike

Sunshine and calm water accompanied our two-hour trip, but the words "gale-force winds" lingered. We rounded the breakwater of the Cape Cod Canal and spotted Sandwich Marina. A gentle breeze carried the scent of fish as we motored past imposing commercial trawlers with towering superstructures and stout hulls. Tim guided *Little Prince* into our slip on the transient dock. I secured the stern line while Tim tied down the bow.

"Did we remember the keys to the house?" Tim asked as he climbed back on board.

I looked sideways at him with a raised eyebrow. "Yes, we remembered the keys to the house. What made you think of that?"

"I don't know, it just popped into my head now that we're hundreds of miles away from the house. Let's walk Tigger and find the showers."

"Yeah, we're due."

The head on *Little Prince* turned into a shower, but I preferred using marina facilities. The showers on the boat required the user to install large plastic panels to form an enclosure. The showers in the marina were larger and easier to use. Long distance boating reminded me of camping. We had some modern conveniences, but a comfortable shower wasn't one of them.

Cleaned and refreshed after our showers, we walked to the harbormaster's office. A navy blue town seal above the portico stood out against the tan clapboards and clean white trim. It read "Town of Sandwich Massachusetts, Incorporated in 1639."

"Good afternoon," Tim said to the harbormaster. "We're here for the night and planning to go to Mystic tomorrow. We read the current can be pretty fast entering Buzzards Bay. Do you have any advice on that?"

"What kind of boat do you have?" he asked.

"A thirty-one-foot Ranger Tug."

"You'll be fine. It's low-powered boats that run into trouble."

"What about the high winds they're predicting? Any updates?" Tim asked.

"If you get an early start, you should be fine. It's not supposed to get bad until late in the afternoon."

We felt moderately reassured and continued back to *Little Prince*. I dug into the cooler and pulled out lasagna. The food had begun to thaw. We needed to purchase more ice for the cooler. With all the cooking I'd done, I wanted nothing wasted.

The canal saved us from the treacherous trip around Cape Cod. George Washington ordered the first of many surveys, hoping to build a canal. It ran east to west and connected the Atlantic Ocean with Buzzards Bay. In the 1800s, tides, shoals, and storms caused a shipwreck every couple of weeks between Chatham and Provincetown off the tip of Cape Cod.

There were several attempts to build a canal, but financier August Belmont II got the job done. Belmont charged ships a toll to recoup his investment but ultimately sold the canal to the United States government for $11,500,000 in 1927, which eliminated the toll. The Army

Sagamore Bridge

Corps of Engineers made improvements, dredging and widening the canal for larger commercial vessels, and continues to maintain it. Every year, thirty thousand ships pass through the canal. We were about to be one of them.

In the morning I threw a sweatshirt on over my PJs, made coffee, and heated water for Tim's breakfast while he walked Tigger. The potent aroma of coffee filled the cabin. Once the water boiled, I poured it into the wide-mouth thermos, along with oatmeal and blueberries, and tightened down the lid. The rolled oats cooked in the thermos. Of all the information I had read about preparing food on a boat, making oatmeal in a thermos proved the most valuable. It became part of our daily routine.

We got underway at 7:00 a.m. The brisk air persuaded me to wait until it warmed up before trading my cozy PJs for jeans. The calm water flowed peacefully as we watched the sun come up behind us, forming garlands of orange and yellow light in *Little Prince's* wake.

Along the seventeen-mile ride, we passed a tug going in the opposite direction and traveled under the Bourne and Sagamore Bridges and by the Massachusetts Maritime Academy. At the Cape Cod Canal Railroad Bridge, the chart showed we were nearing Buzzards Bay. Our plan included crossing the bay and continuing into Block Island Sound and up the Mystic River. Calm water and sunshine made the trip through the canal delightful.

After Wings Neck Lighthouse, the shelter of the canal gave way to open water. The transition started with land on either side, but the distance between the two shorelines gradually increased. As we pulled farther away from land, the water grew choppy. Conditions deteriorated with each nautical mile into Buzzards Bay. The weather report said late afternoon for gale-force winds, but by 10:00 a.m. the growing wind and waves threatened our goal of reaching Mystic, Connecticut, another thirty nautical miles farther.

Weather is one of those things you can't control, along with waves. "Just ride the wave," Rick used to say. He didn't mean it literally, but his words echoed in my head. As we got farther into the bay, the waves and wind continued to amplify. We pushed on, leaving the islands of Cape Cod behind. The moderate protection the islands gave us disappeared, and we were in open water with nothing but the North Atlantic to the east.

By 10:30 a.m., we needed to find a safe harbor, and I needed to do a better job of securing the galley. Six-foot waves pelted the bow, throwing water over the deck and covering the windshield, only to stream off when *Little Prince* rocked the opposite way. A loud thud followed the first sizable wave when a gallon water jug crashed into the aisle. Next, the metal thermos clanged as it hit the floor. A sketchbook on the galley table and a basket of paint brushes followed. Tigger clung to the side of my seat for shelter. While *Little Prince* was being rocked by the waves, I white-knuckled the safety bar so I, too, wouldn't end up on the floor.

We needed to find a sheltered waterway, a river or cove, to escape the pounding seas. I flipped through the chart book, looking for the nearest place of refuge. Tim mentioned the Sakonnet River. I found

it on the chart ten nautical miles away. It relieved me to know there
would soon be an end to the turbulence. Unlike the roller-coaster ride
we had encountered when we headed into the waves, this time beam
seas hit the side of the boat. A constant barrage of swells seesawed
the boat back and forth during the hour it took to get to the Sakonnet.

"She's a very seaworthy vessel," our neighbor Bob had said. I kept
playing those words over in my head as the waves laughed at my
fears. Bob's words were reassuring. When we headed into waves and
smashed down into the troughs, I feared the boat might break apart.
I didn't think it likely, but the doubt terrified me. The beam seas in
Buzzard's Bay heaved *Little Prince* from side to side like a demonic
metronome. I worried we might tip over, even if not a likely scenario.
Regardless of the source of my fear, it had become my regular state
of being.

Finally, we caught sight of the mouth of the Sakonnet. Up ahead, a
small boat anchored near the river concerned us.

"What's that up ahead? Is he okay?" I asked when we were close
enough to see a man fishing off a small boat. Tim maneuvered close
enough for the man to signal if he needed help. Nothing, no sign of
distress, just fishing.

"You've gotta be kidding me! Why would anybody find that fun?"
I said.

"I don't get it either."

Tim changed course and navigated up the Sakonnet River. What
had been beam seas now became following seas, pushing us up the
river. We rode to the crest of each wave and surfed down the backside.
Tim's steady hand on the wheel and knowledge of boat handling got
us to safer water. Three miles upriver, the waves of Buzzards Bay
receded.

I found a marina in the guidebook, and Tim radioed for a slip. We
entered and found boats wedged into a small area. Tim tried to steer
Little Prince against the current into an assigned slip but without
success. Shallow water and the stone breakwater left little room to
maneuver. As if the conditions on the bay weren't bad enough, the

challenges of this marina compounded our stress. We decided to exit and look elsewhere for a place to stay.

As we turned to leave, the current forced us toward the bows of the docked boats. Tim increased speed to move away from them and fight the current. The protruding anchor from a sailboat caught a small railing on *Little Prince*. A thud, a brief grinding sound, and then a splash.

"Shit. What was that?" Tim asked.

I went out the back of the cabin to see. A small railing to the flybridge was gone. The snagged railing had dropped into the water. There was no way to retrieve it.

"It was the little railing to the flybridge," I reported back to Tim.

"Shit. Let's get the hell out of here."

Across the river, we found the Standish Boat Yard in Tiverton, Rhode Island, a much more accessible marina.

Tim pulled up to the fuel dock, and I handed Ken our bow line. Once secured, Tim stepped onto the dock, and Ken, the owner, greeted us warmly. His unmistakable New England accent filled the air. *Little Prince* gobbled up the diesel fuel.

"Could we stay here until the weather clears?" Tim asked.

"Shoah, the weather's gonna get wicked tonight, whippin' up some good waves out in the sound, I heah," he said.

"Yeah, we had following seas pushing us up the river too," Tim told him.

"Last summah, a boat flipped stern ovah bow. A kid drowned under it befoah the coast guard got to 'em."

Well, isn't that icing on the cake? Upending the boat hadn't entered my head. Now I had something new to fear.

"Will this side dock work for you? You can stay long as you need," Ken said, turning around and pointing to the adjoining dock in the working boat area. "Theah's a powah post right theah."

"That would be great," Tim responded.

It was perfect. After fueling up, Ken took hold of our lines and skillfully pulled our boat around to the other side of the dock. I watched in awe as he took the bow line in one hand and the stern line in the other.

Then, with the lines over his shoulders and a few twists and turns, he maneuvered *Little Prince* into place, like a jitterbug dancer guiding his partner around the floor with grace and athleticism.

Ken and Tim secured the bow and stern lines on the cleats. My silence told Tim the day's events had taken their toll on me.

"Do you want me to walk Tigger?" he asked.

"Yes, please." Emotionally exhausted, I had nothing left.

The waning hours of the day became gray and cloudy. So many things raced through my head as the sun began to set. The day had started out beautifully, then turned into a horror show. I had fancied myself the queen of adventure until I sat in a boat, in a strange place, overwrought and hoping Tim would return. We hadn't yet gotten out of New England, and we had so much farther to go. It was October 19 and getting colder every day.

Admitting my fear out loud and regretting my enthusiasm for this expedition was unacceptable to me. I don't give up. I run up to that line that separates brave from foolish and watch it blur. When I bought the house in Hampton Falls and started the renovations, friends used the word brave. Maybe, but I needed to follow my path. Once again, friends spoke of my bravery in making this trip. I was petrified. It may give me pause but not stop me.

After some time, I saw Tim's phone on the table. Panic struck. I stepped outside the cabin and stood in the back of the boat. The darkness consumed the water below as isolation set in. The stress of the day shook me to my core. In my addled state, time blurred; I didn't know how long Tim had been gone. What if he had been hit by a car or broke his leg or, or, or . . .

CHAPTER 27

MUTABILITY

It is the same!—For, be it joy or sorrow,
The path of its departure still is free;
Man's yesterday may ne'er be like his morrow;
Nought may endure but Mutability.
—Percy Bysshe Shelley

In the darkness, I heard Tigger's collar jingle, accompanied by Tim's footsteps on the dock. Relief washed over me, rousing me from the fog of fear that had surrounded me in their absence. I looked along the rail of the boat. When Tigger saw me, he picked up his pace. That fuzzy boy possessed a magical quality that smoothed out the rough edges of my life with a swish of his tail. Tim picked him up and passed him to me.

"Don't you ever leave this boat again without your phone."

"Oh, yeah, when I was crossing the parking lot, I noticed I'd forgotten it."

I glared at him and shook my head. Tim had no notion of the frenzy of anxious thoughts seeing his phone had caused me. He saw my dismay.

"Okay, okay. I'll take it with me next time."

❋ ❋ ❋

Things didn't seem as scary or desperate once the sun came up, but it was October 20. The cloudless sky and chilly air hoodwinked us into believing our journey might continue. I put on a jacket, attached Tigger's leash, and confronted the raw air.

The hulking boat lift, with its arcs of thick canvas, hung over the edge of the water. Boats "on the hard," in varying stages of readiness for winter, encroached on the parking lot. Some were shrink-wrapped, and others waited for power washing.

Tigger and I returned to the boat. I reported the location of the bathroom and showers. Tim sat at the galley table with his laptop.

"Listen to this." Tim read the marine forecast off his computer: "The National Weather Service in Boston/Norton has issued a Gale Warning, which is in effect from 2:00 p.m. Wednesday to 8:00 a.m. Thursday. Winds and seas: West winds fifteen to twenty-five knots, with gusts up to thirty-five knots. Seas four to seven feet . . ."

"Are we ever going to get out of New England?"

"I had to order a charging cord from Amazon. I forgot to pack mine."

"When will it get here?"

"Tomorrow. I should go up to the chandlery and let them know it's coming. After I read the weather warning, I knew we had the time."

I poked around our provisions for breakfast offerings. A package of blueberry scone mix filled the bill. I added a cup of water, mixed the thick batter with a fork, dropped four large spoonfuls onto the cookie sheet, and slid it into the oven. The four dollops of batter filled the sheet made for our undersized oven. On the counter, at the other end of the galley, just behind the captain's chair, I readied our four-cup coffee maker with grounds and bottled water and switched it on. The rich scent of coffee brewing blended with the sweet aroma of the baking scones. The cabin of terror became cozy and warm.

A marine store occupied the back of the main building, near the street above. As we entered, I noticed three men on worn-out chairs in a corner of the room, drinking coffee from paper cups, uniformly dressed in flannel shirts and work boots. They looked as though they regularly congregated there. It reminded me of Mert Dyer's drugstore in Peterborough. A group of similarly dressed older men often gathered around a table in the front of the store. I found it comforting. It felt like home. Time stood still in Tiverton but not in Peterborough. After Mr. Dyer sold his store to Rite Aid, the men no longer gathered there.

I wandered up and down the aisles while Tim spoke with Ken's wife behind the counter. Some items looked like permanent fixtures covered by a layer of dust that had accumulated over time. I like marine shops the way I like hardware stores. They're full of things you don't realize you need until you do. It's then they became a shining beacon of salvation.

Somewhere between the wing nuts, cotter pins, and cup hooks, a packet with bright red letters jumped out at me. Kill switches, eight of them in the package, one for every kind of outboard motor, including ours, for $6.89. I brought the packet to Tim. By now, Judith had already shipped ours to New Jersey. We bought them anyway.

Later that afternoon, Tim stood on the dock watching a large boat pull up to the fuel dock. He hovered in the area to assist, if needed, although it appeared Ken had the situation well in hand. Ken pulled the stern line to tie it up. Splash! Without warning, Ken slipped and plunged into the water. The yacht continued to move closer to the dock and threatened to crush him. Tim went into action, grabbed the boat railing, and pushed it away from the dock, giving Ken room to scamper up the ladder.

I heard the commotion and stepped outside in time to see Ken step off the ladder onto the dock. He returned to his work and didn't slow down. Everyone on the boat and dock urged him to change his clothes, but he insisted he was fine. We looked at one another in astonishment at Ken's resistance to the chill. He finished the task at hand, dripping wet in fifty-degree temperatures. Ken completed the transaction before he walked up to his house for a hot shower and dry clothes.

When the commotion ended, I took out my sketchbook and

watercolors. I drew a weathered post draped with ropes that I could see from the galley table window. The rumble of the boat lift cranked up from time to time to haul another boat from the water.

Night came, and the cooler full of prepared meals proved invaluable. Even if we wanted to eat out, we were miles from everything. The stove warmed the cabin as dinner cooked. Outside, the temperature dropped. Before bed, Tim checked the dock lines in anticipation of the high winds.

At midnight, thirty-five mile-per-hour wind gusts jolted us awake. The wind screamed and growled. *Little Prince* convulsed with each blast as the dock lines shrieked under the strain. We couldn't sleep. We lay there and listened to the wind assault the dock lines. The blows kept coming.

"Are you awake?" Tim asked around 3:00 a.m.

"Yeah."

"We may need to come up with a plan B if we don't get a break in the weather."

I lay there, silent. The wind continued to howl.

"Like what?"

"We could have the boat hauled and trailered. Marinas are closing for the season. It's something to think about."

The wind died down, and we fell back to sleep.

Morning came, and we turned on the marine forecast. Waves were expected to reach heights of ten to fifteen feet in Block Island Sound. A full week into the trip, and we were only in Rhode Island with no hope of continuing that day. We wondered if our adventure might be doomed.

Our delays pointed to another problem. Tim had brought a limited amount of warm clothing. He thought we'd be further south by now. Ken generously offered the use of his car so we could go into town. We found a shopping center and looked for a hat and some warm socks for Tim. We ate lunch at a little place on the highway. A taste of civilization helped my state of mind. I picked up another scone mix and some other provisions at the grocery store.

Fueled up, wastewater pumped out and provisioned, we needed a break in the weather. Day four of our stay at Standish Boat Yard arrived. The weather cleared enough to head out. It was sunny and thirty-eight degrees at 7:30 a.m. We cruised down the Sakonnet River into Rhode Island Sound. The crisp morning promised significant progress.

We traveled close to shore to see the historic mansions of Newport, south of the Sakonnet. Some of these "summer cottages" were private residences, and others, museums.

"Look at that one. It must be a municipal building," I called out as we passed a brick building that dominated the coastline with its six chimneys and multiple peaked roofs. The mansions grew larger as we moved along. I tried to imagine the parties thrown by the Vanderbilts or the Astors. Each one trying to out glitz the other.

We hoped staying close to the land would help with the choppiness of the water and allow a better look at the mansions. The recurring theme that seemed to be the hallmark of our adventure persisted. The longer each day went on, the stronger the wind. Six-knot winds rose to seven and continued to twelve knots. My ability to secure the galley improved, but the rough water always tossed *Little Prince* around enough to find something to hurl onto the floor.

Tim turned on all four windshield wipers at top speed to counter the waves splashing over the bow. A rush of water yanked one wiper from its base. It dangled in front of Tim's windshield unfettered, a vanquished soldier.

When Tim and I saw Fishers Island on the chart, we hoped it would give us shelter from the gusts. The wind wasn't deterred. The waves grew, and we hung on tight. Five hours into our trip we worked our way toward the mouth of the Mystic River. Waves crashed against the hull. Up ahead, we saw a small boat bobbing like a bathtub toy.

Tim and I looked at each other.

"What is wrong with these people?"

"I don't know what it is about fishing that people are so attracted to," Tim responded.

Just like at the mouth of the Sakonnet, a man in a small boat held tight to his fishing pole as the waves bounced him up and down.

Tim maneuvered around Fisher Island Sound to the Mystic River. Once in the channel, the course curved between Ram Island Shoal and Morgan Point then guided us around Swimming Rock and Planet Rock. The well marked channel required an attentive captain.

We continued up the river and reached calm water. Tim radioed ahead for a slip. I looked forward to this stop because friends Mark and Diane lived nearby. Diane had helped me get through the last several years. I had met her when I'd moved to Peterborough, more than twenty-five years earlier. After Diane had married Mark, a Navy man, she moved to Connecticut. She and Mark put us up every year I participated in the Mystic Outdoor Art Festival.

When I applied to the Mystic show years ago, I doubted I'd be accepted. The show drew thousands of people because of the fine quality of the artwork. When the jury approved my application, it thrilled me to be part of such a well respected show. I knew other artists in the show and felt honored to be in their company.

As we waited behind another boat for the Mystic River Railroad Bridge to open, I wondered how close we were to downtown, where the Mystic Outdoor Art Festival took place. We passed through the open bridge, and I watched it close behind us. I felt secure. The rough water could no longer reach us as we pulled into the marina. Dockhands signaled our slip assignment. As Tim lined up *Little Prince*, they grabbed the bow line and pulled us in.

Little Prince secured, Tigger stared up at me wagging his tail. He didn't need to speak. I knew what he wanted and attached his leash. No one enjoyed reaching land more than Tigger.

CHAPTER 28

MYSTIC

Life is the art of drawing without an eraser.
−John W. Gardner

We walked up the ramp to the packed dirt parking lot. Scrub and over-grown weeds along the edge led to a dumpster. A boat that would never touch the water again lay on its side nearby. Another boat, supported by jack stands, towered above the ground. A hull of chipped paint and exposed wood looked exhausted, a shell of its former glory. The far corner of the lot opened to another area filled with boats on the hard.

The marina's restaurant, Red 36, occupied prime real estate on the water. The crisp white trim, wraparound deck, fashionable wicker chairs, and paved parking lot contrasted with Seaport Marine's build-ings next door. As a repair and maintenance facility, its engine parts, tools, and broken boats told the story of the work needed to keep boats afloat.

Out on the street beyond the boatyard, we saw a park with new playground equipment and an attractive black metal fence that kept the children safe. The smell of green grass replaced the scent of die-sel exhaust and salt air. On the corner stood a sun splashed apart-ment house, a hundred years old or more, three stories tall with white clapboards. Flower boxes on the porch railing overflowed with red and yellow blossoms.

Another park, lined with trees and benches, buffered the riverwalk from the shops and traffic. As we continued to walk, I recognized the street. Several of my artist friends had displayed their work there during the art show. I looked around as though staring at my past. Robin set up her booth on this street. Her exquisite still life paintings impressed onlookers and judges. Steve displayed his striking New England landscapes next to Robin. The tents that filled the street then were long gone.

The shops and riverwalk were familiar, but I was different. The dissonance between my past and present had reached a critical juncture. I realized my experiences made my life richer. I traveled an ever-changing path, full of high winds, low tides, and smooth seas. All of it was part of my journey. I had held onto my grief long enough. Feeling guilty for being happy no longer haunted me. Grit and determination had gotten me to this confluence, and now the two parts of my life no longer collided but instead flowed together. The turbulence subsided. The importance of the Mystic show, once a milestone in my art career, faded into my past.

For the first time, I no longer felt like a stranger in my own life. The weight of uncertainty that had dominated my thoughts for years began to lift. I didn't know the future—no one does. Our journey on *Little Prince* embodied the unpredictability of life. We cannot prevent pounding waves or create fair winds, but we can decide when to set sail and when to seek safe harbor. We walked into Mystic Knotwork and bought Tim a blue and white reef knot boutonniere for our wedding.

Saturday morning, the marine forecast predicted wave heights of fourteen to twenty feet. Small craft warnings went into effect. I didn't want to know what twenty-foot waves would do to *Little Prince*. Regardless of the weather, we planned to spend the day in Mystic.

Mark and Diane came by.

"Hey, Barb," Diane said as she walked down the dock. "How are you guys doing?" she asked with a smile and a gleam in her brown eyes.

"Just swimmingly," I responded, and we broke out in laughter.

After the vexing start to our journey, seeing familiar faces breathed new life into my weary spirit.

"This is a nice rig," Mark said as he and Diane stepped on board *Little Prince*.

While I was showing them around the boat and the electrical panel, Tim stepped in and flipped the switch that said, "head lights." Tim and I looked at each other, and I hung my first mate's head in shame. Ever since we had left Portsmouth Harbor, I couldn't understand why the bathroom lights didn't work.

I had followed Darren's instructions at Badger Island Marina. I turned everything off. Tim plugged us into the power post on the dock, and then I turned on everything we needed. Repeatedly, I stared at the electrical panel, trying to figure out why the bathroom lights didn't work. When Tim reached in and flipped the switch, I realized that head lights were bathroom lights. I felt pathetic.

The sunny weather allowed us to sit outside—wearing sweatshirts. The bench seat at the stern finally got some use. Smaller seats on either side made *Little Prince*'s exterior the perfect place to sit and visit with Mark and Diane before heading out for dinner and provisioning. The now empty cooler had served its purpose, and we needed to refresh our food supplies.

Mystic's history of shipbuilding goes back to the 1600s. Nineteenth-century shipwrights built more than six hundred vessels along the Mystic River. The tradition continued with the restoration of the *Mayflower II*. The project began in 2016 as a cooperative venture between Plimoth Patuxet Plantation Museums (they use the old spelling), guardian of the *Mayflower II*, and Mystic Seaport. We had been disappointed when we couldn't see the *Mayflower II* in Plymouth and made a point of returning to see the restored ship a few years later.

The restoration involved using lumber from live oak and white oak trees. Durable and rot resistant, live oak is curved like the lines of a ship. Mystic Seaport acquired live oak after Hurricane Katrina had damaged trees in Louisiana. In Belle Chasse, Louisiana, twelve live oak trees needed to be removed because they blocked the path of new power lines. Another live oak in Pass Christian, Mississippi, sustained damage during a lightning strike. The families knew the value of the wood for old ship restoration and donated the lumber to the shipyard.

To restore the *Mayflower II*, shipwrights used a mix of old and new tools, like adzes, broadaxes, hand planes, and chisels. They manipulated caulking rope between boards with mallets and caulking irons to keep the ship watertight and structurally sound. Lumber for the hull required the use of power tools. The shipwrights preferred white pine for masts and cedar for planking. They learned their craft through apprenticeships at Mystic Seaport.

Two years after our journey, the British Consul General to New England christened the restored ship with water from all fifty states, England, and the Netherlands. The *Mayflower II* then sailed down the Mystic River, through the Cape Cod Canal, with the aid of tugboats, and back to Plymouth. The same route we had taken, in reverse.

Throughout our trip, I posted updates on social media. I felt like I had friends joining us as we traveled down the coast. After I posted about arriving in Mystic, Kevin, an old family friend, replied to my post, "We just passed Mystic!" They were on their way to Providence, Rhode Island, and heading back to New Jersey on Sunday. The marine forecast called for ten to fourteen-foot waves in Long Island Sound on Sunday, so we weren't going anywhere.

On Sunday morning, a sheet of ice covered the dock. In the afternoon, Kevin and Eileen stopped by on their return trip. Later, Tim called Mike Rizzo to keep in touch and seek advice about approaching weather. He and his wife had left from Rhode Island by boat heading to Florida as well. Mike's experience boating in these waters comforted us. Somewhere along the way, we hoped to meet up with them.

It wasn't to be. Mike and his wife also took a pounding from the high winds and waves on Long Island Sound. They found shelter at a marina in Connecticut that was shutting down for the season. The Rizzos opted for plan B. They rented a car and returned to Rhode Island. The next day, they pulled their boat from the water and trailered it, setting out for Florida by land.

On Monday, the weather improved enough to tackle Block Island and Long Island sounds. We planned to make it to Port Chester, New York, or at least Greenwich, Connecticut, where Tim grew up. As a teenager, he'd operated the launch for tips at the Old Greenwich Yacht Club. He ferried people out to their moored boats in a large rowboat with an outboard motor.

The Mystic River Railroad Bridge lifted, releasing us from the security of the harbor. Sparkles of morning sunshine danced on the river. The busy intersecting roof lines of Mystic gave way to green lawns and maple trees beginning to change color. Stately New England houses dressed in white clapboards or cedar shingles reigned over the river, along with private docks and moored sailboats. At Morgan Point Lighthouse, we entered Block Island Sound and continued to Long Island Sound.

Our morning routine of boiling water and pouring it into a thermos with oatmeal returned. A breakfast bar filled my needs. Making lunch became a challenge. More than once, one hand held on for dear life while the other made sandwiches.

Our trip into Long Island Sound followed a familiar pattern. The sunshine deceived us; wind and waves kicked up again. We thought as we got farther into the sound, Long Island would block the wind and help lessen the waves. It didn't work out that way. Waves continued to worsen as the day wore on. The tension of another bout with rough water caused my body to stiffen. Our chances of getting down to Port Chester or Greenwich looked grim.

"When is this trip going to be fun?" I asked Tim.

"I wish I knew. Once we get to the ICW, it should be much better, but we still have a ways to go before that."

"And Hell Gate."

"I don't think we'll have a problem with Hell Gate as long as we time our entry with the tide."

"And we don't meet up with any barges."

"It'll be fine," Tim tried to reassure me.

I tried not to think about all I had read about Hell Gate. I pushed it out of my mind and watched as dark clouds formed. Our sunny skies morphed into partly cloudy, then became mostly cloudy. With all the time we'd had in Mystic, I had secured things in the galley so Tigger wouldn't have to dodge water jugs or plastic cups sliding off the counter. Once again, I played the words of our neighbor Bob over and over in my head: "It's a very seaworthy vessel." And once again, we needed a river for shelter.

CHAPTER 29

HELL GATE

Security is mostly a superstition. It does not exist in nature,
nor do the children of men as a whole experience it.
Avoiding danger is no safer in the long run than outright exposure.
Life is either a daring adventure, or nothing.
–Helen Keller

Still in Connecticut, we selected the Branford River for our safe harbor. Fifty nautical miles from Mystic, we landed at Brewer Bruce and Johnsons Marina. Chris, the dockmaster, helped Tim with pointers on docking. Our neighbor in the next slip, Joey, with a heavy New York accent, sang Chris's praises as a docking coach.

"I bought this in Jersey," he said with a sweeping gesture of his boat. "I didn't know a thing about boats when I drove it here. Chris taught me how to dock. He's the best."

"What about Hell Gate?" I asked.

"Oh, it's nothin'!" Joey said.

With his lack of experience and our taking all the precautions we could, I was oddly reassured.

During the 1800s, Hell Gate caused nearly one thousand ships to run aground, sink, or become damaged every year. Rocks, especially

Pot Rock, caused the most damage to ships but now no longer threatened boats. In 1852, a 125-pound charge blasted Pot Rock, along with the man who had placed the charge. Engineers blew up more rocks over time, and passage became safer. The Army Corps of Engineers continued work on the East River, including Hell Gate's Pot Rock. The Corps blasted it again in 1885 and dredged the channel.

Along with the shipwrecks came legends of sunken treasure. In 1780, the HMS Hussar went down after striking Pot Rock. For 150 years, treasure hunters looked for gold, allegedly on board, to pay the British soldiers during the Revolutionary War. With all the blasting and dredging in succeeding years, if there had been gold on board, it landed in the landfill on Long Island. We still had a couple of days before that challenge.

The tide could be five or six knots. Underpowered vessels, like sailboats, can run into trouble. Various sources recommended slack tide, between high and low tide, as the safest time to traverse the narrow passage. I had my copy of the tide charts handy, so we would know the best time to go.

In the morning, we refueled and pumped out the wastewater, ready

Execution Rock Lighthouse

to head down the Branford River and on to New York. We planned to stay at a marina near the East River to time our foray into Hell Gate.

Finally, a delicious day awaited us, oozing with sunshine and garnished with puffy clouds. We passed a red tugboat, half a dozen tires hung from the side of the bow. On Long Island Sound a pale blue tug pushed a barge transporting a crane. The calm water hosted all manner of working boats. We cruised diagonally across Long Island Sound. I followed our progress, displayed on the chartplotter screen, and there it was, Gardiner's Bay, on our port side. One of my favorite Billy Joel songs played in my head. In it, he mentions the bell in Gardiner's Bay. I grabbed my phone, turned on the Bluetooth speakers, and cranked up "The Downeaster 'Alexa.'"

That song always moved me. The crescendo of the music, and the story of the Long Island fishermen losing their way of life, had a poignancy I couldn't escape. The places named in the song, always somewhat familiar to me, now took on a new meaning.

We didn't need to be in rough water to feed our family, like the fishermen in his song. We pulled into a safe harbor when we felt uncomfortable. The choppiness we encountered didn't come close to the fierce conditions fishermen battled. Billy Joel sang about the need to travel more miles away from shore every year to find fish. I had gotten a hint of what that meant as well. As the music played, I observed the activity with a new appreciation for life on the sound.

Several more bays carved out from the shore of Long Island dotted the chart: Smithtown, Huntington, and Oyster Bay. Off our starboard bow, Stratford Shoal Lighthouse sat alone on a little island, also called Middle Ground, because it sits five nautical miles from New York and five and a half nautical miles from Connecticut.

Explorer Adriaen Block (from whom we get the name Block Island), first identified Stratford Shoal in 1614. The shoal eroded until it hid below the surface of the water. Buoys marked the dangerous spot, then lightships. When a location was too difficult for building a lighthouse, a lightship identified the hazard. The first Stratford Lightship off the shoal dragged its anchor several times during storms. In 1877, the federal government allocated funds to add rocks, make a small island, and build a lighthouse.

In 1905, Gilbert Rulon, the main lightkeeper, went on shore for supplies, leaving assistant lightkeepers Julius Koster and Morrell Hulse unattended. The desolation of the lighthouse drove Koster mad. In Rulon's absence, Koster tried to cut Hulse with a razor. A few days later, Koster jumped off the tower into the water. Hulse jumped into the water and saved Koster. Rulon sent the troubled assistant back to the mainland where he committed suicide. After that, lightkeepers claimed the spirit of Julius Koster haunted the lighthouse.

After World War II the coast guard began automating lighthouses to save money and avoid the isolation and hazardous conditions some lighthouses presented. In 1968, the Coast Guard accelerated the program. It automated Stratford Shoal Lighthouse in 1969.

Through the haze, a tiny New York skyline peeked up from the horizon. Tim radioed ahead for a slip in Port Washington, New York, the perfect location for our descent into Hell Gate.

Tim navigated between Sands Point and Execution Rocks into Manhasset Bay. The name Execution Rocks may have come from unproven tales of British soldiers chaining colonists to the rocks to drown as the tide came in. Or, perhaps people who had watched from the shore as ships crashed on the rocks gave them their name. Eventually, Congress allocated funds to erect a lighthouse.

The gruesome past of Execution Rocks continued into 1920. Charles "Carl" Panzram, a serial killer and lifetime criminal, used the area as a dumping ground for the bodies of ten men he had murdered while in New York. Overnight visitors have reported hearing footsteps and seeing apparitions in Execution Rocks Lighthouse.

We followed the channel into the bay and pulled into a slip. Marina employees used golf carts to get around the concrete docks that spanned the width of a city sidewalk and traversed a mile of distance. We plugged into shore power, but only one line worked. We asked the dockmaster about it, but he couldn't help. Tim called Mike Rizzo for suggestions. He talked about the inverter, and my eyes glazed over. I took pictures of the lights on the inverter, and we sent them to Mike. We also had a technician from the marina look at it. No one seemed to know what ailed *Little Prince*.

We stayed an extra day at the marina because of the high winds. If it weren't for all the warnings about Hell Gate, we might have continued. Based on the tides, we wouldn't be making an early start. At 11:00 a.m. on Thursday, October 25, we exited Manhasset Bay and headed for the East River and Hell Gate.

After rounding Hewlett Point, we passed Little Neck Bay. Ahead of us, Stepping Stones Lighthouse marked the channel entering the East River. The glare of sunlight on the water created a hazy view of the Manhattan skyline, framed like a toy city below the Throgs Neck Bridge.

I watched a red barge the size of a small ranch house advancing on our port side. The open water provided plenty of room as the barge forged ahead toward Long Island Sound. After passing under the bridge, we had little room to maneuver. Seeing the barge reminded

Brooklyn Bridge

me of the material I'd read about the danger of encountering large commercial vessels in the narrow passage.

Throgs Neck Bridge soared above *Little Prince*. Corpulent metal cable swooped down between arched towers and dropped vertical strings anchored to the deck, like an immense Celtic harp. The road-bed carried six lanes of Interstate 295. The vertical clearance of 142 feet left ample room for boats to fit beneath the bridge. Throgs Neck, a peninsula in the Bronx, protruded into Long Island Sound and formed a boundary with the East River. The narrow opening to the East River provided the perfect place for the imposing bridge.

When I saw the name "Throgs Neck Bridge," I flashed back to traffic reports I'd heard as a child. NewsRadio 1010—my mother's favorite station—gave a traffic update every fifteen minutes. Before school, as I munched down my bowl of Cheerios, I often heard, "Traffic is jammed up getting on and off the Throgs Neck Bridge." Forty years later, we cruised under the bridge I had often heard about but never seen before. New York City, Hell Gate, and seven more bridges awaited us.

Tides ruled the flow of the East River, technically a tidal estuary. Water poured in from the Atlantic Ocean or discharged from Long Island Sound with whatever force Neptune decided for the day. The ocean and the sound played tug-of-war four times a day, heaving the water back and forth through the narrow strait. Our safest opportunity for passage came at slack tide.

We entered the East River and watched a plane take off from nearby LaGuardia Airport. Next, the Whitestone Bridge came into view. Each bridge became a gateway between the past I had left behind and a future that once seemed uncertain. It all converged on this turbulent waterway.

CHAPTER 30

LADY LIBERTY

Give me your tired, your poor,
Your huddled masses yearning to breathe free,
The wretched refuse of your teeming shore.
Send these, the homeless, tempest-tost to me,
I lift my lamp beside the golden door!
—Emma Lazarus

The river narrowed. The current picked up speed, and the radio crackled, ready to warn us of oncoming boats. To starboard, Manhattan Island dominated the scene. Buildings filled the horizon with no daylight between them. Angled roofs intersected the squares, rectangles, and spires of adjoining buildings. Mirrored exteriors reflected blue skies and old red brick buildings reminded us of the city's age.

I stepped outside to take pictures. The sweet smelling air carried none of the stale scents of the city, choked with the exhaust of buses, cabs, and delivery trucks. We were outsiders peeking into the world of luxury apartments, hustling street vendors, and multimillion-dollar business transactions.

On the opposite side of the East River, houses and trees lingered until we approached Rikers Island and New York City's infamous

189

prison. The New York Department of Corrections turned the island into a prison in 1932. Inmates at Rikers served short sentences or awaited bail hearings. With a long history of being exceptionally violent, Rikers loomed ahead of us, isolated and foreboding.

Tim followed the clearly marked channel around Brothers Islands to Wards Island where the river narrowed and Hell Gate Bridge arched overhead. Its towers looked menacing as they came into view above the surging current. Urban legend claimed the lights of a ghost train appeared to approach the bridge but never crossed. The train, they said, carried the one thousand plus souls who had died in 1904 when the ship General Slocum caught fire and sank in the water below. It was New York's worst tragedy until the attack on the World Trade Center on September 11, 2001.

We passed under the Robert Kennedy Bridge and entered Hell Gate, the one-mile stretch of water I feared most. We cleared Wards Island and turned starboard, where Hallets Point blocked the view of any oncoming vessels. No warnings of oncoming ferries, tugs, or barges came over the radio. The Harlem River surged into the East River as we left the point behind. The water convulsed as the two rivers

Statue of Liberty

merged, and the channel narrowed further around Roosevelt Island. Churning water and whitecaps surrounded *Little Prince*. To starboard, a whirlpool off Mill Rock spun around like the skirts of a twirling ballerina. Waves, swirls, and boils diminished but didn't stop. The slack tide limited the force of the unruly water. My fear and anxiety subsided as *Little Prince* powered through the agitating water of Hell Gate, and Tim handled it all.

I had spent too much time worrying about what could go wrong. With Hell Gate behind us, our trip turned magical. Roosevelt Island lay in the middle of the East River. More bridges, with greater than one hundred feet of clearance, spanned the river. Paul Simon's "The 59th Street Bridge Song (Feelin' Groovy)" played in my head as we passed under the Queensboro Bridge, also named the 59th Street Bridge. I'd walked around that area on a visit to my brother Joe's first apartment in New York.

Our readings also warned of an area where the subway tunnel ran beneath the river and caused unexpected turbulence. Whirlpools and eddies appeared in different places on the East River. In Tim's boating experience turbulence normally signaled danger from rocks close to the surface. Our reading ahead of the trip alerted us to the peculiarities of the East River and quashed any fears the chaotic water might have caused.

We spotted familiar buildings among the mass of concrete, steel, and glass. The Chrysler and Empire State buildings stood out with their familiar profiles. My favorite, the Chrysler Building, with its shiny arches and Art Deco design, pierced the sky. For eleven months it held the title of the tallest building in the world—until the Empire State Building surpassed it.

The farther we went, the better it got. We still needed to be alert, but fear no longer dominated my thoughts. The unique perspective from the water made the familiar appear different. The idea of Manhattan Island being small always puzzled me. How could so large a city be on such a small island? That confusion cleared as we cruised alongside the banks and saw it from the water perspective.

After another bend in the river, we were looking at two more bridges. We passed under the Manhattan Bridge, then the Brooklyn Bridge, the granddaddy of them all. It connects City Hall in Manhattan with Brooklyn's Fulton Ferry Landing. The stone neo-Gothic structure that John Roebling designed remains one of the most recognizable bridges in the world. The first fixed bridge to span the East River, it opened in 1883 and made the list as a National Historic Landmark in 1964 and the Register of Historic Places in 1966.

A few blocks from the river's edge stood the Freedom Tower, its sleek glass and metal exterior contrasting with the architecture of the Brooklyn Bridge. As beautifully designed as the Freedom Tower is, it didn't prevent memories of the day terrorists attacked the World Trade Center to come flooding back. Three members of my family worked in the vicinity, and it took several hours to learn they were all safe. The New York skyline I knew growing up included the World Trade Center. Its absence brought a profound sadness, but I put those feelings aside.

An unexpected visual treat followed. The sight of the Battery

New York City Sykline

Maritime Building, a Beaux-Arts building erected from 1906 to 1909, caught me off guard. It's a ferry terminal and beautiful. Three archways accommodated the ferry boats. An ornate exterior of embossed rosettes, nautical symbols, and geometric patterns decorated the archways and columns. The striking facade incorporated rolled steel, copper, zinc, cast iron, and cobalt blue tiles. In keeping with the original color scheme, the interior arches were pink. The details and workmanship in the design made it a hidden gem seen only from the water. The behemoths that surrounded the terminal lacked the elegance of the Battery Maritime Building. The terminal shut down in 1938, but in 2001 a restoration project started. The deteriorating building became a luxury hotel with elegant restaurants and a jazz club.

New York Harbor, also referred to as Upper New York Bay, opened up in front of us—to starboard, the southern tip of Manhattan, to port, Governors Island. Once a military post dating back to 1776, Governors Island became a recreational area only reached by ferry. There are no longer any permanent residents, but free cultural events take place on the island.

The busy harbor mirrored the streets of New York City, bustling with ferries, tour boats, pleasure and working craft. The Staten Island Ferry passed by. Across the bay, a British aircraft carrier, the HMS Queen Elizabeth lay at anchor. Its size, of three football fields, dwarfed the passing ferry boats.

The pinnacle of our expedition through New York Harbor came next.

The sight I had most looked forward to seeing, the Statue of Liberty, stood before us. I had been looking forward to this part most of all. Twice I'd climbed to the crown. One summer day, after my first year at Northeastern University, I took the train into New York City with my mother to have lunch with Aunt Mary at the Seamen's Church Institute restaurant. Aunt Mary loved the food there, but then Aunt Mary liked hospital food too. After lunch, she returned to work while my mom and I walked around Battery Park.

"I wonder where that goes," I said.

"What?"

"See that boat? Let's see where it goes."

Reluctantly, my mom agreed, and we took the boat out to the Statue of Liberty. Years later, I did the same with Rick and our sons on a trip to the city. When we returned to my parents' house, my mom asked where we had gone.

"The Statue of Liberty," Rick replied.

"She didn't drag you to the top of that too? She made me climb up it when I was an old lady."

My fondness for the lady with the torch went beyond those visits. In 1910, at eleven years old, my grandfather came to the United States from Ireland, aboard the Caledonia. Authorities on Ellis Island processed Grandpa Mike, his father, two older brothers, an older sister, and two younger sisters. I wondered if he saw the Statue of Liberty when they entered New York Harbor. I wondered if his picture hung on some wall or in a book that displayed immigrant boys dressed in wool coats and herringbone flat caps. Where Tim's family came on the *Mayflower*, mine were among the masses that sailed into New York Harbor "yearning to breathe free."

I never made it to Ellis Island when I lived in New Jersey, but we could see it in the distance. The flow from the Hudson River contributed to the changing currents, but the width of the harbor allowed the energy to dissipate. While I took pictures of the Statue of Liberty and Lower Manhattan, a clipper ship sailed by. Everything fell into place. All the worry and fear melted away as we marveled at the views.

CHAPTER 31

NEW JERSEY

There are some things you learn best in calm, and some in storm.
—Willa Cather

Our last bridge for the day, the Verrazano Narrows Bridge, connected Staten Island and the Bronx over the Narrows of Lower New York Bay. The succession of bridges, all different, felt like the final gauntlet of my battle to let go of the past. Each bridge served a purpose, solved a problem, and represented the architecture of its time. My bridges were people. On our journey, whether by fate or happenstance, I connected with friends important to me at every stage of my life.

I posted a picture of the Statue of Liberty on social media as we headed for Atlantic Highlands, tagging two old friends. Good luck continued to make it a wonderful day. Both friends responded. Forty years had passed since I last saw Susan, a friend from grammar school. I didn't know what to expect.

We cruised under the bridge to the Jersey side. Our struggle to leave New England ended as we pulled into a slip at Atlantic Highlands Municipal Marina, Sandy Hook Bay, New Jersey. Tim plugged in our power cords, and everything worked fine. The problem we had encountered in Port Washington had nothing to do with *Little Prince*: It had been the marina's power post.

When we docked, I rushed to the showers. I needed some freshening up after life on the boat. Susan came by. As I exited the ladies' room, I saw her sitting on a bench, looking out toward the water. From behind, I recognized her blond hair, and when she greeted me, her brown eyes transported me back in time. Recollections of our school days at St. Joe's, Girl Scouts, and hot summer days at the community pool came into focus.

I refused to let the awkward question about kids dampen our brief visit. As we walked down the dock toward *Little Prince*, I quickly told her, "I just wanted to tell you, I'm widowed, and my son died of an overdose."

"Oh, Barb, I'm so sorry."

"Thanks. I just wanted to get that out of the way. I usually lie to people when I first meet them and say I have just one son, but I didn't want to do that with you—and I didn't want to spoil our visit with depressing stuff."

"I understand," she said with the same smile I remembered. We climbed on board *Little Prince*. Sue put out her hand and introduced herself to Tim, and we went on chatting like schoolgirls again. The afternoon flew by as hazy memories and current life events brought our two lives together again. Sue wished us well in our journey, followed the dock to the parking lot, and receded from view.

Kerry, a friend from college, also lived in Atlantic Highlands. She recommended a restaurant, and we met her there for dinner. As though no time had passed, we chatted away the evening. We had talked on the phone in recent years and caught up on family life, but this was the first I'd seen her since Richard's baptism. Kerry was Richard's godmother.

Both these ladies had grown up to be professional women, and the way they presented themselves to Tim struck me. Immediately offering their hands and formally introducing themselves. I wondered if I had returned to New Jersey and worked in New York, would I also have developed a more professional demeanor? Our dinner together capped off a fabulous day. At the end of our visit, Kerry gave us a ride back to the marina.

Time and turbulence changed my perspective. The weather cooperated, the East River cooperated, and the views of New York from the water made this leg of our journey the best we'd experienced. The horrors of Hell Gate belonged in the past, along with a lot of the other fears and uncertainty I carried with me. This adventure, however harrowing, brought internal calm. I was present in my life, and seeing old friends and family had helped put me there.

The sky turned crimson as the sunset. "Red sky at night, sailor's delight; red sky in the morning, sailor take warning." The old sailor's adage assured us of another beautiful day on the water. New Jersey had its own Intracoastal waterway, and we just needed one more day of open ocean travel to get to it. In two days, a nor'easter would arrive.

The morning greeted us with partly cloudy skies and sunshine bouncing playfully on the ripples in the water. Sandy Hook Point marked the entrance into the Atlantic Ocean as we headed south along the New Jersey coastline. A fishing boat farther out attracted a flock of seagulls. Tim easily navigated the calm water. It wasn't a long trip to the Manasquan River, but with the nor'easter coming, we wanted plenty of time to get settled at a marina before it hit.

As long as we stayed sheltered, I wasn't too concerned. After New Hampshire, a nor'easter without snow didn't seem too frightening. Those storms could drop a few feet of snow on the ground. Everything came to a standstill with that much accumulation. I liked the quiet aftermath of a snowstorm, but I didn't know what to expect from a rain nor'easter.

By noon, we were on the Manasquan River, passing beneath Route 35, a familiar road to anyone who's been to the Jersey Shore. We traveled up the river and came to Clark's Landing Marina in Point Pleasant. It looked like a fine place to stay and wait out the storm. We backed into our slip, plugged in our power cords, and stepped out onto our finger dock. The narrow finger docks alongside the boat at Clark's

Marina felt like a gymnast's balance beam. Once tied up, we walked through the parking lot to the street in search of lunch. I looked at the street sign: "Arnold Ave." My parents had retired here, and Arnold Avenue was the town's shopping hub. We walked a few blocks and found a deli.

A lot of places call themselves a "deli," but if I weren't in New York or New Jersey, I wouldn't bite. My heart skipped a beat when I saw "Sloppy Joes" on the menu. Town Hall Delicatessen in South Orange had the best sloppy joes of my youth, but there's no such thing as a bad deli sandwich. A New Jersey Sloppy Joe didn't include ground beef. Prepared with rye bread, turkey, roast beef, Swiss cheese, coleslaw, and, finally, Russian dressing that oozed out, dripping off your hands. Sloppy and wonderful, it screamed New Jersey. The food, the accents, and the overall familiarity of the place recharged my confidence.

We wrapped up what we couldn't finish and headed back to the marina. No need to worry about dinner. Our leftovers covered that. We doubled up on our lines, walked Tigger, stocked the fridge with wine, and waited for the storm. Swells in the river hinted at the storm to come. Tim adjusted the stern lines a second time to keep the dinghy from hitting the dock. In rough weather, the lines needed special care. He worked to achieve the right balance between enough slack to rise and fall with the tides and swells but secure enough to prevent the boat from banging against the dock.

As evening turned to night, the wind and waves escalated. The marina offered scant protection as the nor'easter blasted the coast a couple of miles east. The relentless howling kept us awake as *Little Prince* gyrated between the pilings. Rain battered the deck. The storm crawled up the Atlantic like a lumbering beast. Daybreak revealed a submerged dock with high tide still an hour away. We nixed our plan for my brother, Jim, to drive us to the store for provisioning.

I called to let him know.

"Can you come by tomorrow instead of today?"

"Sure, why?"

"The dock is underwater, so we can't get off the boat."

"No shit," he said, chuckling. "Power's out all over the shore, all kinds of flooding and trees down, I guess."

By midafternoon, the water had receded, and we took Tigger for a walk. My cousin Betsy came by for a visit in the afternoon and brought a large pork roll (or Taylor Ham, if you must). Once upon a time, you could get pork roll only in New Jersey. Getting an entire roll from Betsy was a special New Jersey treat and would be served at many breakfasts on our trip.

Once the storm blew over, things were fine the next day. Jim came and brought us a bottle of champagne and the kill switch. We'd been rocking and rolling so much for nearly three weeks, our legs were unaccustomed to dry land. Jim drove us to a grocery store, and we stocked up on supplies. Our trip continued the next morning.

CHAPTER 32

DELAWARE BAY

If your ship doesn't come in, swim out and meet it.
—Jonathan Winters

The Manasquan River connects to the Point Pleasant Canal, then to Silver Bay and Barnegat Bay. Although calm water flowed through the inland waterway, depth became a problem. Names of places familiar to me appeared on the chart as we moved through each successive bay. The shallow water in Barnegat Bay surprised me. Tim needed to stay in the channel and keep a sharp eye on the depth finder.

Barnegat Lighthouse, at the north end of Long Beach Island, weathered this nor'easter just as it had every storm for more than one hundred fifty years. It stood at the inlet between Long Beach Island and Island Beach State Park. I had climbed the stairs to the top of "Old Barney" as a child. The National Park Service listed it in the National Register of Historic Places in 1971. The Coast Guard decommissioned the lighthouse, and it became the property of New Jersey and part of a state park. To me, it looked like an old friend.

As we passed under the causeway that connected LBI to the mainland, I remembered driving over it every summer and the big moment when we could smell the salt air. My parents rented a house for two weeks on the southern end of the island. Every day we'd go to the beach, jump the waves or ride them on rubber rafts, and enjoy the sun and water. I spent the most carefree days of my life on LBI.

The highlight of our vacations came when Dad rented a boat so we could go fishing on the bay. It felt like a grand adventure. All six of us, my parents, three older brothers, and me, piled into a small outboard and went out on the bay for the day. My dad knew nothing of boating, but that never stopped him. He was a veteran of World War II, a radio operator on a B-17 Flying Fortress. Nothing scared him, or so it seemed. He went to college on the GI Bill and became a successful businessman. He commuted into New York City every day. I never remember him taking a sick day, though I couldn't swear to it. "Big Joe" was a formidable character, but on boating day, he was as much of a kid as we were.

It shocked me when the water depths in Barnegat Bay required Tim's attention. The little girl in me still thought we were out in the deep blue sea. The wind and swells kicked up. We'd been at it for more than five hours and were making good progress, but the shallow water of the inland route made it slow going, something to think about.

Morrison's Marina came into view a short distance ahead. We arrived at three o'clock with time to wander around. The bad news: Morrison's Restaurant (home of my favorite clam chowder) had burned down. We walked up to Bay Avenue, the main street that traverses the island. I looked around and saw familiar sights. On the opposite corner from Buckalew's Tavern stood Kapler's Pharmacy. The facade hadn't changed, with one exception. A large mortar and pestle protruding from the front of the brick building that bore the pharmacy's name had an addition, a web address. A block away, the market used to have a donut making machine in the window. Tim became hostage to my trip down memory lane.

"Tim, we have to go this way, just a block. I have to see if the donut machine is still there."

"What?"

"At the market. They had the best donuts."

Unfortunately, the machine was no longer there to tempt passersby, but I'd never forget biting into the warm, fresh pillow of goodness and the sugar crystals that cascaded down my chin. I'd lick my lips over and over to get every bit of sweetness. My disappointment softened with the thought that nothing is ever as good as we remember from childhood.

Regardless of the temperature, in the mid-fifties, and with the sun descending, I needed to go to the beach. The closer we got, the stronger the scent of salt air. A couple more blocks east, the magic of the dunes captivated my imagination. Somehow, the gentle slopes of sand covered in beach grass hid the ocean and buffered the sound of crashing waves. Weather-worn steps brought us up and over the dunes. I paused at the top of the stairs, intoxicated by the salt air and entranced by the rhythm of the waves. It felt like a gateway to the best days of my childhood.

Wispy clouds and the soft light of the setting sun took me away. I wanted to be that little girl again, if only for a moment, and enjoy the simplicity of life when my greatest decision was to determine how far back from the water to build my sandcastle. Too close, and the water would destroy it before I finished; too far, and I'd need to haul water to pack the sand.

"You ready to get something to eat?"

Tim's voice dragged me back to reality. I knew I couldn't sit in the sand, watch the waves, and wander through time the way I wanted.

"Sure."

"Where to?"

"Buckalew's. Not much else is open. Most places shut down by the end of September."

After dinner and a short walk back to *Little Prince*, we planned the next day. We weren't the only people making the journey down the coast by boat. Other people making the trip posted information about conditions on a social media page. I had been following the posts and chatted with a few people online since we had left Plymouth, Massachusetts. The shallow water of the inland waterway urged caution and a slow pace. We considered going back out into the ocean so we could make better time getting to Cape May, New Jersey.

In the morning, online acquaintances reported calm water ahead. They were in a sailboat, so water depths determined their route. A sailboat requires more water because of the keel attached to the bottom of the boat. With those assurances, we decided to go back out to the ocean when we reached the southern tip of Long Beach Island.

Carefully staying within the channel, we went south toward Little Egg Inlet. Around the tip of LBI, the channel narrowed, and we headed into the waves. Suddenly, each wave pulled the water out from underneath us, causing the depth alarm to go off. The water churned and crashed around us in a frenzied fandango of whitecaps, breakers, and swells, trying its best to push us out of the channel, each time setting off the depth alarm. Tim constantly shifted his eyes from the waves to the depth monitor to look for deeper water. Running aground felt like a real possibility and could damage the boat.

"Shit, are those rocks up ahead?"

"No, there aren't rocks here," I told him, but with each sound of the depth alarm, his responses became more colorful.

Finding deeper water was critical. The depths on either side of us ranged from one foot to five feet. *Little Prince* needed three feet. Then, almost as quickly as the tumult came upon us, we were in twenty feet of water. The waves went from breaking to choppy and continued to settle. The jarring episode lasted twenty minutes and registered as the most frightening leg of the trip. We quickly learned the dangers of entering and exiting inlets.

Out in deeper, calmer water, we traveled at ten to twelve knots. The morning scare turned into a lovely afternoon of cruising. With the temperature nearly sixty degrees, the cold weather of New England faded into memory.

We arrived at the Cape May Inlet after lunch. A stone jetty protected the inlet from rough water. Off our bow, a dolphin led the way. The inlet led to a well-protected harbor with several marinas, restaurants, commercial fishing operations, and the United States Coast

Guard Training Center. Utsch's Marina, at the opening of the Cape May Canal, looked like a good place to spend the night. We didn't yet know that the weather gods had decided we would be in Cape May for four days.

The southernmost tip of New Jersey, Cape May is where the Atlantic Ocean meets Delaware Bay. It's the country's oldest seaside vacation spot and is known for its collection of Victorian houses. The National Park Service designated the city a National Historic Landmark in 1976. By the mid-eighteenth century, it was a popular vacation spot for people traveling by schooner, stagecoach, and horse-drawn wagon. Major fires hit Cape May in 1856 and 1878. The second fire destroyed thirty-six buildings. During rebuilding, the original Victorian style was retained.

We would be staying at least another day, thanks to the marine weather forecast. We took advantage of the bike rentals at the marina and zigzagged through town to see all we could. Bric-a-brac bedecked the exteriors of the houses painted in a variety of colors. Corbels, dentil molding, and running trim decorated the roof lines, while ornate balusters, handrails, and newel posts adorned the porches. House after house, street after street, all followed the same pattern of colorful, well appointed houses.

The weather cleared, and on November 4 we said goodbye to New Jersey. There would be no more familiar places, no more friends and family to help with provisioning, just me, Tim, Tigger, and a pile of charts. Each leg of this journey felt like an echo of the last few years. I had moved to Hampton Falls without knowing a soul there. In the same way, the calm waters of the Cape May Canal gently eased us into foreign territory. The three-mile waterway cut across the southern tip of New Jersey, linking up with Delaware Bay. Inhaling the fresh, cool air, I pretended to be in a familiar place. I'd crossed the Delaware River numerous times and had worked as a camp counselor near the Delaware Water Gap, two hundred miles north of us. I clung to that feeble connection for as long as I could.

Like the Cape Cod Canal, the proposal to build the Cape May

Canal came long before construction began, first in 1808. They drew up plans without result, then more plans, and then President Franklin Roosevelt vetoed a bill funding construction. Next, Congress passed a bill without funding. The impetus to begin work on the canal happened in 1942 during World War II when German U-boats torpedoed dozens of boats off the New Jersey coast. A sharp turn at the entrance of the canal prevented German submarines from entering Cape May Harbor and provided safe passage for American ships. For us, it was a pleasant shortcut.

I rubbed the back of my neck as we approached the ferry terminal and the hulking vessels waiting to transport cars and people. Tim followed the channel markers into Delaware Bay. I turned around and watched New Jersey melt into the past. There was no turning back time or *Little Prince*.

CHAPTER 33

CHESAPEAKE BAY

My world has changed, and so have I.
I have learned to choose and I have learned to say goodbye.
—Pocahontas

A stout red lighthouse brought my thoughts back to our adventure. It cautioned boaters of Miah Maull Shoal, named after a riverboat captain. In 1780, Miah Maull left Delaware on a ship bound for England to claim a substantial inheritance. He never made it. The ship crashed into the shoal, and Maull drowned. At an auction in 2015, the lighthouse sold for ninety thousand dollars.

We passed barges, tugboats, and Ship John Shoal Light. A ship traveling from Germany called John, went aground on the shoal on Christmas Eve 1797. The rescued passengers spent Christmas with strangers in the area.

The moderate swells lessened when the bay narrowed. We navigated north fifty-two nautical miles to the Chesapeake and Delaware Canal starting at Reedy Point in Delaware. That ditch is fourteen miles long and saves three hundred miles of travel between Philadelphia and Baltimore. As a merchant in Philadelphia, Benjamin Franklin favored building the canal. Like other projects, there were proposals, plans, and funding issues. The completed canal opened in 1829.

It took 2,600 men to dig the ditch with picks and shovels. The average daily wage amounted to seventy-five cents. At first, teams of horses and mules towed schooners, sloops, and barges through the waterway. Over the years, expansion accommodated more traffic. Steam powered boats and millions of tons of cargo required periodic improvements, which continued until the 1970s.

Regardless of the substantial impact on commerce, I liked the short-cuts and smooth rides the inland waterways provided. In 1824, a pump powered by a waterwheel controlled water levels. Today, electronics perform the same function. As we cruised the C&D Canal and headed for Chesapeake Bay, everything familiar disappeared.

After eighty-seven nautical miles, we ventured up the Sassafras River to the Georgetown Yacht Basin and secured a mooring. It was quiet, calm, and peaceful, and we hoped for a few more such days.

In the morning, mist rose from the surface of the water. The air smelled of autumn as leaves fell from the oak trees along the river-bank. We needed to lower the dinghy and take Tigger for his walk. Tim got the key for the lock securing the dinghy and tried to unlock the chain. The frozen lock stayed shut. We tried WD-40, but it wouldn't budge. Once again Rose, the dinghy, presented a problem. Tim explained our situation to the dockmaster, and he retrieved a pair of bolt cutters.

We refueled and cruised down the Sassafras River to Chesapeake Bay. We thought the rainy weather would clear. Conditions deterio-rated closer to the mouth of the river. Waves continued to grow as we entered the upper Chesapeake Bay. After two hours, we looked for a place to stay.

We anchored *Little Prince* in Worton Creek, twenty-four miles south. Contrary to what I had once thought, the mariner doesn't just throw out the anchor. I learned the process in one of the boating courses I'd taken: Drop the anchor line several lengths longer than the depth of the water, also known as "scope," and back the boat up until the anchor catches on the bottom. Tim was familiar with the process, but we had practiced only once with *Little Prince* in Maine.

The extra line allowed the boat to swing some with the tide but not move beyond that. Too short a line created the risk of dragging the anchor. An anchor alarm provided an extra safety precaution. If the boat moved farther than the range you set, the alarm sounded. We picked a spot far enough away from other boats and started the procedure. After several tries, we thought we had it right. This was our first overnight on the anchor. We had time before we went to bed to hear the alarm sound if we didn't properly set the anchor.

In the morning, the drizzle and fog continued. The white house at the end of the walkway that had caught my attention the day before looked more alluring in the fog, like something out of *Gone with the Wind*. After we got up, a man from the marina came by in an outboard and told us we were too close to the neighboring boat. We weren't as secure as we'd thought. Tim moved farther away from the neighboring boat and prepared to launch the dinghy for Tigger's walk.

Tim got into Rose, and I handed Tigger to him. Tim gave the pull

The Dismal Swamp

cord on the motor a tug, then another. It sputtered but didn't turn over. A couple more pulls, and out came the oars. Life with Rose continued to present problems. Once Tigger completed his mission, we moved on. Our questionable anchoring prowess made us eager to leave. We needed to keep moving as much as possible. We forged ahead.

The conditions in Worton Creek were tolerable—drizzling and choppy. Out on the Chesapeake, fog set in. The fog became denser as we moved along.

"Whoa," I said as a crab boat appeared through the curtain of fog.

"Yeah, I didn't see him at all," Tim responded. "This isn't safe. If this doesn't clear up soon, we need to pull in somewhere."

Besides the crab boats, we were the only jackasses on the water. It reminded me of the lobstermen in Maine who worked in the foulest conditions. The sun didn't burn off the fog. A little farther on we called it quits.

Rock Hall Harbor, Maryland, provided safe harbor. A narrow channel with a concrete breakwater on either side was problematic in the fog. It surrounded the harbor like a medieval castle's walls. The channel markers were difficult to see. Tim guided *Little Prince* to Rock Hall Landing Marina, and we settled in for the day. With our early start and quitting after only three hours, a 10:30 a.m. arrival provided time to explore.

When evening approached, the faint smell of fried seafood from Waterman's Crab House, next door, drifted our way. The scent lured us in for an early dinner of crab cakes. Tall windows looked out onto the harbor. Outside seating was closed for the season. We had come very far, but the calendar didn't lie. It was November 6 and chilly.

After dinner, during the short walk to our slip, we saw a rainbow.

"That's gotta be a good sign," I said to Tim.

"I hope so. We're running out of time. The marine forecast said we'll have two good days ahead. We should be able to make it to the ICW by then."

To the west, the sunset turned the sky bright orange. The rough morning turned into a beautiful evening. Day twenty-eight was ending with 650 nautical miles behind us, no more North Atlantic, a favorable weather forecast, a rainbow to the east, and a gorgeous sunset to the west. Favorable omens overflowed, we thought.

We awoke to a beautiful, sunny morning, just like the weather report had promised. I filled the coffee maker with water and grounds, turned it on, and then walked Tigger. Tim reviewed the chart. When I returned, the smell of fresh coffee permeated the cabin. Our traveling routine continued as I microwaved some water for Tim's oatmeal and set it aside in the thermos to cook. Leaving Rock Hall Harbor without fog simplified our exit. The formidable cement breakwater that gave pause when we were entering the harbor looked like a friend waving goodbye under sunny skies. A good night's sleep, a positive outlook, and a yearning for more progress took hold.

On the Chesapeake, we cruised at ten to fifteen knots, with no fog or shallow water. We passed the usual array of barges and tugs. After an hour, we passed under the Chesapeake Bay Bridge. The burned out wreckage of a large ship appeared off our port side. It looked like it might break in two because of extensive damage two-thirds of the way aft from the bow. An eerie quality surrounded it. We didn't get any closer. It looked dangerous, and we were making good time.

Suddenly, boom! A tremendous bang reverberated through the air. The boat slowed to a crawl. I was sure the engine had exploded.

"What was that?" Tim asked.

"What happened?" I asked in return. Then I saw Tim's hand on the throttle slowly bring *Little Prince* up in speed.

"I thought we hit a rock," Tim said.

I realized Tim had slowed the boat when we heard the explosion. It wasn't the engine. We were fine. The Patuxent River Naval Air Station, not far away, tested supersonic military aircraft to make sure they reached the speed of sound and to confirm their speed. The locals were aware of this phenomenon. We were not. If we had become complacent with the great conditions, the sonic boom woke us up.

We approached the Potomac River and looked for a marina. After six hours on the water, the time to call it a day had arrived. Smith

Point Marina, near the mouth of the Potomac, looked promising. We crossed the border between Maryland and Virginia and entered Captain John Smith country.

The Jamestown Settlement, located less than a hundred miles south, launched Captain Smith into history for reasons other than his exploits with Pocahontas. While at Jamestown, he traveled three thousand miles and mapped the Chesapeake Bay area during expeditions in 1608 and 1609. The accuracy of the map he created received high praise in England because of the benefit to future explorers. In a 1616 voyage, he mapped out Northern Virginia and renamed it "New England." The pilgrims purchased his map before they left for their journey on the *Mayflower*.

In 1612 Smith wrote his first book, which included his map of Chesapeake Bay and extensive notes about people, nature, and geography. He wrote a follow-up book in 1624 and went into greater detail. The second book was the first reference he wrote about Pocahontas, which cast some doubt on the legend.

With another eighty-nine nautical miles behind us, Tim radioed ahead and received more instructions on how to get to the marina. Creeks and coves emerged along the way as the river rounded several promontories.

Dan, the owner of the marina, greeted us at the dock.

"Are you okay with the outer dock, instead of a slip?" Dan asked.

"Sure," Tim responded. "We'll only be here for a night."

"You'd better check the weather," Dan responded.

"Oh no. We thought we had two good days ahead," I replied.

"There's been a change in the weather forecast," Dan replied.

After we tied up, plugged in, and walked Tigger, I checked the weather. Dan was right. It was bad.

NAVIGATIONAL CHARTS *

(continued)

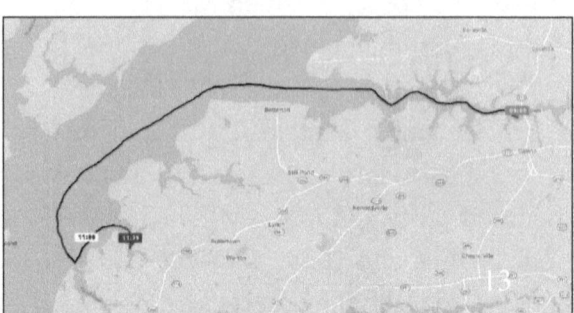

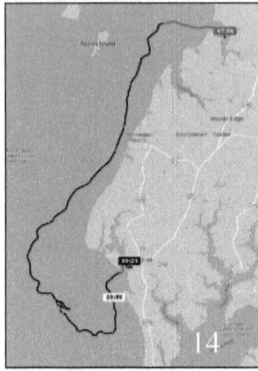

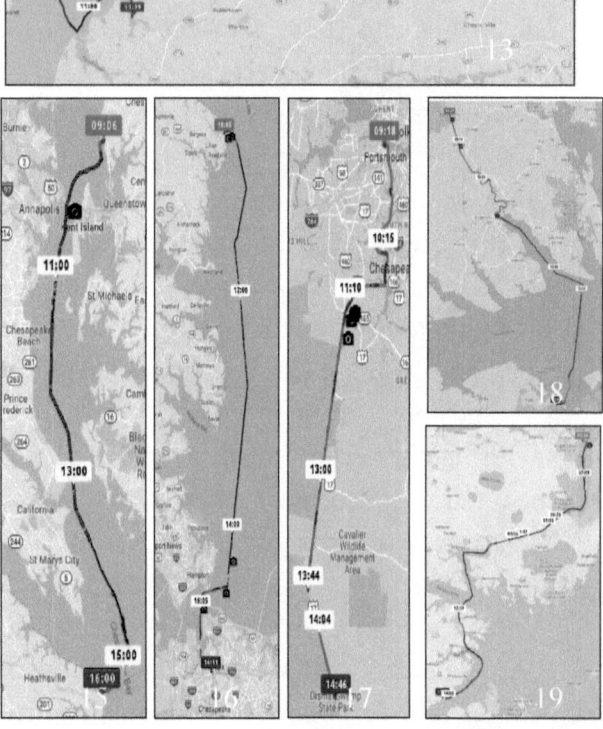

13.) Georgetown, MD.
to Worton Creek, MD

14.) Worton Creek
to Rock Hall, MD

15.) Rock Hall, MD
to Smith Point, VA.

16.) Smith Point, VA.
to Portsmouth, VA.

17.) Portsmouth, VA. to
Dismal Swamp, N.C.

18.) Dismal Swamp, N.C.
to Alligator River, N.C.

19.) Alligator River,
N.C. to Oriental, N.C.

20.) Oriental, N.C. to
Sneads Ferry, N.C.

21.) *Sneads Ferry, N.C. to Southport, N.C.*

22.) *Southport, N.C. to Myrtle Beach, S.C.*

23.) *Myrtle Beach, S.C. to Georgetown, S.C.*

24.) *Georgetown, S.C. to Charleston, S.C.*

25.) *Charleston, S.C. to Beaufort, S.C.*

26.) *Beaufort, S.C. to Savannah, GA.*

*Note: To see larger images in color go to https://barbarabusenbark.com/charts/

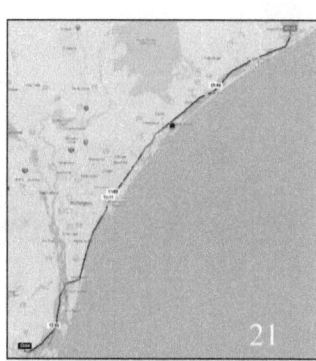

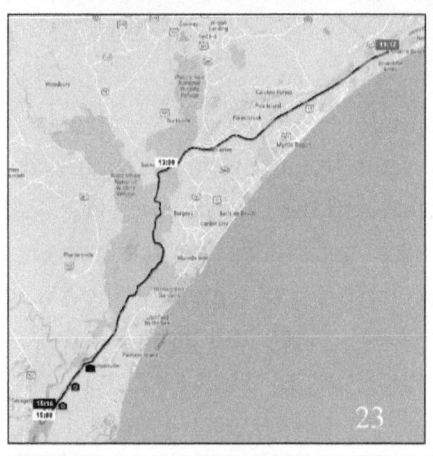

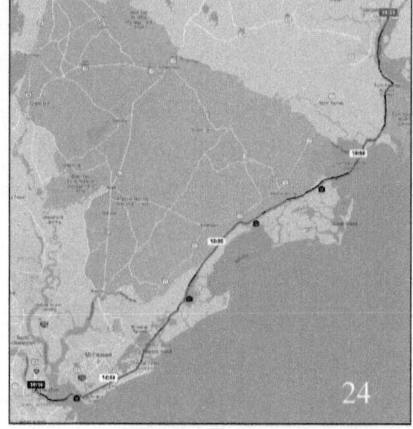

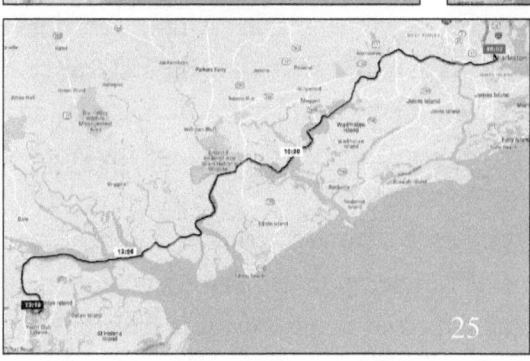

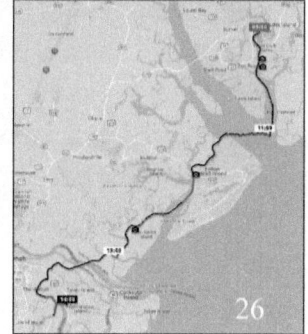

CHAPTER 34

THE GREAT DISMAL SWAMP

Damnation seize my soul if I give you quarters, or take any from you.
—Edward "Blackbeard" Teach

After three days of pounding rain and high winds, the weather cleared. Portsmouth, Virginia, awaited us. Thimble Shoals Lighthouse marked the entrance to Hampton Roads Channel and the Elizabeth River.

The Norfolk Naval Station is situated at the entrance to the river. After my late son, Richard, had completed his deployment on the *USS Enterprise*, Rick, Mike, and I drove down to pick him up in Norfolk. Memories of Richard took over my thoughts as we passed massive navy vessels. *Little Prince* felt like a bathtub toy as we cruised by foreboding, gray hulls the size of shopping plazas. Aircraft carriers reminded me of Richard proudly showing us all around the Enterprise. Like everything else, he did it with energy and enthusiasm, rushing from one area to the next, words pouring out as he explained the workings and function of everything on board.

I kept my thoughts to myself as we moved along. I could never explain to Tim my feelings or every memory that took me back in time. There are some things you can't fix and some thoughts that remain buried within our souls. I knew we'd be seeing something of where

Richard was stationed, but the vast navy presence awakened the pain of his death. Everything overwhelmed me: the ships, the docks, the cranes, everything.

Erratic messages from the GPS brought me back to the present. It took only a few seconds to realize the naval station had caused the interference. We assumed the navy had jammed any transmissions, and we made our way to Portsmouth. We stayed at a marina a short distance from the ICW.

In the morning we continued our journey. A sign, "Mile Post 0" firmly planted along the banks of the canal marked the entrance to the ICW and the Great Dismal Swamp. A line of boats waited for the Norfolk and Portsmouth Belt Line Railroad Bridge to open. After that, a fork in the canal presented two routes: the Great Dismal Swamp Canal or the Albemarle and Chesapeake Canal. We knew the Dismal Swamp was the slower route but also more scenic. We stuck with our plan, the swamp route.

The Great Dismal Swamp, like the other canals we'd traversed, played a role in the early development of the East Coast's waterways. It connected the Chesapeake Bay via the Elizabeth River in Virginia to the Pasquotank River and the Albemarle Sound, North Carolina. Work on the canal began in 1792 and ended in 1895. The oldest manmade canal in the United States, the twenty-two mile waterway is maintained by the Army Corps of Engineers.

Engulfed in a canopy of trees, the narrow passageway lay before us. The moist air enhanced the colors of the leaves along with the scent of decaying foliage. Soft yellow pastels mixed with greens while naked branches poked through the mosaic of color like the flailing arms of a clumsy dancer. Unlike the brilliant autumn colors of New England, the leaves made a subtle shift in hue. Reflections from a thin layer of clouds formed a soft runway down the center of the canal.

The water on either side of the strip mimicked the dark greens and browns of the dense woods. Murky water and dark reflections made it impossible to see below the surface. Tim slowly guided *Little Prince* through the shallow water, while we kept a lookout for submerged logs. Quiet and calm, the canal contrasted with the angry waters of the North Atlantic we had faced at the beginning of our journey. I no longer needed to grab hold of the bar in front of me, or so I thought.

We approached Deep Creek Lock in time for the next opening. In preparation for this trip, I had read about the locks. Mariners seemed compelled to relay horror stories in explaining the process of passing through them. The most alarming warned that without enough line, your boat will be suspended in the air when water surges out of the lock. Tales of nasty lockmasters didn't help either. We lined up behind the other boats and threw our lines up to the dockmaster. He closed the gate behind us, filled up the lock, and opened the forward gate—and we were off. Once again, my fears were unfounded.

Behind the North Carolina Welcome Center, a dock accommodated boats traveling the ICW. Because of limited space on the dock, boats "rafted up" for the night. The first vessels to arrive tied up to cleats on the bulkhead until full, and the next boat tied up to the first column. As late arrivals, we were in the third and final column.

Rain dampened the evening. Our neighbors were an older couple who had traveled from Germany in their sailboat. They asked if we'd be leaving early in the morning to make the first opening in the next lock. We said we were and relieved their concerns about missing the opening.

The particularly awkward part was Tigger. To get to land, we walked across two boats, our immediate neighbor and their other neighbor tied to the dock. I'd felt funny enough walking across someone else's deck, but throwing the dog into the mix added more unease. We kept it to a minimum. There were other people with dogs, just not our neighbors.

As promised, we left at 7:30 a.m. A line of boats motored out at the same time to catch the South Mills Lock for the posted opening time of 8:30 a.m. Another cloudy, gray day awaited, but a temperature of sixty degrees made it comfortable. A gauzy mist hovered on the surface of the slow moving water.

The lead boat in our convoy alerted us of dangers ahead on the open channel of the radio. Every once in a while, we'd hear something like, "Just bumped into a log on the starboard side."

We reached the South Mills Lock, whose lockmaster, Bob, doubled as the drawbridge tender farther down the canal. A man with a sturdy build, Bob had a weathered complexion that broadcast the amount of time he had spent outdoors. He wore an orange vest and a long sleeved flannel shirt. As water filled the lock, Bob got on the radio and called the lead boat's name, followed with, "Captain, y'all lemme know when you're fifty yards from the bridge."

"Roger that," the lead boat captain responded.

The lock gates opened, and we followed along in single file. After a few minutes, we heard Bob again on the radio.

"Captain, do y'all see the bridge yet?"

"Yeah, but we're still a hundred yards away."

"A hundred yards? Boy, I don't know where y'all learned measurin', but I sure hope you don't play football," Bob shot back.

A couple of minutes passed before the lead boat radioed back, "Okay, we're fifty yards now."

"I gotcha," Bob responded. "Lemme know when the last boat's through."

"Yes, sir," came from the last boat.

After our bit of comic relief from Bob, the serene beauty of the swamp again took hold as we continued on to Albemarle Sound. I soon realized my belief that nothing but smooth waters lay ahead turned out to be premature. After passing ICW mile marker seventy, we entered the open water of Albemarle Sound. The grab bar in front of my seat came in handy once again. We just needed to get across to the Alligator River.

Our bumpy ride ended at the Alligator River Marina, a short distance from the mouth of the river. We arrived on Tuesday, November 13, at 2:00 p.m., after traveling fifty-two nautical miles in seven hours. We settled into our slip. A sailboat arrived a short time later and struggled with backing into the slip next to ours. The captain's traveling companion had bailed out on him a couple of days earlier. That thought set my mind racing. No, I couldn't do that to Tim, could I?

The Alligator River Bridge next to the marina swung open at 7:30 a.m. for the parade of boats headed south. The canal traversed the Alligator River National Wildlife Refuge. Expansive areas of wetlands, with a profusion of grasses, marshland, and trees, covered the land leading up to the Pungo River and Pamlico Sound. Shrimp boats docked on Gale Creek appeared as we approached Pungo River, each of them with spars on either side that reached up as high as the muscular hulls were long, fifty feet or more.

A great deal of pirate activity had taken place along this stretch during the eighteenth century. North Carolina provided a haven for the pirates. The many creeks and inlets we passed made excellent cover for them.

Blackbeard started out as a privateer, which meant he had "papers" from the English government, allowing him to attack and pilfer ships from France and Spain during Queen Anne's War. He captured his ship, Queen Anne's Revenge, from the French. The privateers assisted the crown as mercenaries and sent some of their revenue back to England. When the wars between the countries ended, the privateers didn't want to give up the money and became pirates, without the blessings and protections they once had.

Charles Eden, governor of North Carolina from 1713 to 1722, befriended Edward Teach, Blackbeard. The pirates seized merchant ships coming to trade or sell their cargo, stole the merchandise, and then sold it at discounted prices to the colonists. For the governor and citizenry, the situation worked fine. For those states selling and trading with North Carolina, it was unacceptable.

The pirates careened their ships every few months, meaning they purposely ran aground onto a beach to clean and repair the hull. Blackbeard had no fear of capture in North Carolina, so he sailed *Queen Anne's Revenge* into Pamlico Sound to set up a base on one of the islands and careened his ship. Virginia wanted to put an end to the piracy North Carolina ignored. The governor of Virginia knew

Blackbeard planned to set up a fort on Ocracoke Island in Pamlico Sound and sent two sloops to confront him.

On November 22, 1718, Blackbeard and his crew fought a bloody battle with the Virginians. It took five musket balls and twenty knife wounds to kill the infamous pirate. Almost to the day, three hundred years later, we entered Pamlico Sound.

We were no longer in the quiet confines of the canal when the waves kicked up and the cloudy skies turned to rain. From Pamlico Sound, we turned into the Neuse River in search of Orient, North Carolina, a boaterfriendly town with marinas and a free town dock. The shallow water in the Neuse allowed waves to form quickly. The direction of the wind caused conditions to worsen. Water splashed over the bow. As I grabbed hold of the bar in front of my seat, I closed my eyes and promised God I'd stop swearing if he made it stop. My exhausted tolerance for being thrown around by wind and waves pushed me to the breaking point. I opened my eyes periodically to see if things looked any better. I knew closing my eyes equated to a child's sticking her fingers in her ears and saying, "La, la, la, la, I can't hear you," but it helped.

CHAPTER 35

WHAT COULD GO WRONG?

In the end, it's not the years in your life that count.
It's the life in your years.
—Abraham Lincoln

After three hours on the Neuse River, we reached our destination. It was Wednesday, November 14. Inside the harbor, we pulled up to the town dock. The rain had slowed to a drizzle, but more rain was on the way. We made eighty-seven nautical miles that day. The progress felt good, as did being tied up at a dock.

Based on forecasts, we feared we'd be staying another day in Orient. In the morning, the submerged dock confirmed it. I didn't know a dock could be underwater, yet here we were, for the second time in our trip, staring at our boat's fenders floating above the dock, which served no purpose. The water receded as the day wore on, and by evening a beautiful sunset made us hopeful for smoother sailing on the next leg of our journey.

We used the extra time the bad weather provided to make plans. We had an idea of how far we could comfortably go in a day. It made sense to find a marina in the Waterway Guide and make a reservation. Each day, we had gone as far as we wanted, and then looked for a place to stay. That method worked, but given the time, and a better idea of what our days on the water looked like, why not have a solid destination?

Using the Waterway Guide and websites, I found one that seemed particularly nice from the description. Even the name sounded attractive, Swan Point Marina. "Watch the sunset over the water from the Adirondack chairs," it said. "Concierge service to local restaurants." What could possibly go wrong?

As promised, the morning brought sunny, calm weather. We crossed the Neuse River and ticked off mile markers, averaging nine and a half nautical miles per hour. Along the way, a variety of seabirds lined up on the remnants of docks that had succumbed to hurricanes and neglect. The tall grasses along the marshes had turned golden in the crisp fall air and the trees, a dull green. Tim constantly monitored the depth, careful to stay in the deepest part of the canal.

One sign caught our attention near Marine Base Camp Lejeune. It said, "Live Firing in Progress When Flashing." I'm happy to report that it wasn't flashing.

After we entered Howard Bay we began to look for the channel markers that would direct us to Swan Point. A maze of little islands stretched across the shallow water and created the perfect spot for pirates. Dolphins played in the water ahead. A large blue building for boat storage or maintenance came into view. White letters on the front read "Swan Point Marina," along with the white silhouette of a swan. We pulled up to the dock, but no one came out to help. Tim went to find the dockmaster, and I put on Tigger's leash.

As I walked with Tigger, the dilapidated conditions of the dock became more evident. Weathered, uneven boards led to gaping holes, waiting to swallow up any misplaced steps or small dogs. The missing planks revealed rusty nails protruding from the supports below. I veered around the damaged areas, confused and apprehensive. What I'd read on the website didn't match what I saw. Chunks of concrete, rebar, and boat parts littered the ground beside the building. Nowhere did Adirondack chairs or concierge service appear. I got back to the boat feeling deceived. Tim returned, unable to find anyone.

"I'm not getting off this boat again. That dock is terrifying."

"Do you want to leave and look for someplace else?" Tim asked.

"No, it's getting late. I don't want to be out when it's dark."

"All right, but yeah, this is bullshit."

As the sun set, I made deviled eggs. Things always seem better on a full stomach. I boiled water and busied myself in the galley. I tried not to think about the conditions outside. With the eggs cooked and filled, I put them on a plate and turned to place them on the table.

Whoosh!

"Shit!" I yelled.

The eggs slid off the plate, onto the floor. All was not lost. They stayed upright, and I cleaned their little bottoms with a damp paper towel. With that, we sat at the table to eat as darkness engulfed the boat.

Bam, bam, bam. The marina manager's hand slammed the side of the boat.

Tim stepped outside and said, "I hope you're not looking for money."

"Then leave," the man said.

"We're not going anywhere at this hour," Tim replied.

"I'm going to call the cops then," the man responded.

"Good, call them."

Tim followed the man down the dock. Images of an overweight sheriff, spitting chewing tobacco, and wearing mirrored sunglasses, even at night, flashed before my eyes.

Meanwhile, I sat in the boat, looking into the darkness outside and wondering if the police were on the way. Are we going to get evicted? Is there going to be a bigger confrontation, and just what more can go wrong?

I heard footsteps coming toward *Little Prince*. I stepped outside the cabin and saw Tim heading my way.

"Well, we don't have to pay anything," Tim said.

"Huh? What happened?"

"He went inside the building. I thought he was going to call the cops. Then a car pulled up. It was the owner. I told him about the holes in the dock and other problems and the false claims on their website. He said if we weren't happy, we didn't have to pay. The owner probably knew he'd get shut down if the town knew how bad the conditions were. I was hoping he'd call the police."

"Of course you were, but bailing you out of jail wasn't part of the plan. I just can't wait to get out of here."

As soon as the sun rose, Tim fired up *Little Prince*, and we hightailed it out of there. I received a call from the car delivery service. They could pick up my car in Maine and transport it to Florida in three days. I had to tell them no, not yet. We didn't know when we'd reach Gulfport, but it would be more than three days. Another timing issue arose. I had an art show coming up in December in Gulfport, with an opening reception on December 7. The real world started to collide with our never ending trip.

Later that day, we arrived at Southport Marina, the antithesis of the nightmare at Swan Point. Dockhands helped us on arrival. Tim received a welcome packet when he checked in at the office, and he saw a dog park. The warm atmosphere washed away the ill feelings left by our previous experience.

After dinner, we watched the sunset over the Elizabeth River. The orange sky, the earthy scent of sea grass, and the raspy sound of palm fronds created a lovely atmosphere, but time weighed heavily upon us. We needed to make a decision about getting home.

Morning came. I walked Tigger, made a pot of coffee, and cooked Tim's oatmeal in the thermos. As we traveled, we saw an abandoned shrimp boat and stranded pleasure boats. The constant menace of shallow water kept us alert. We knew it would be an issue, but it was evident that not everyone heeded the warnings. We passed acres of marshland, interspersed with driftwood and scrub pines. The tree line in the distance lost most of its color. Herons and egrets stood guard on the water's edge, waiting for their next meal.

As we moved along, my phone rang. Our neighbor in Florida let me know the post office wanted to resume our mail. I told her where we were and that it would be a while before we got there. She relayed the information to the mail carrier. Another reminder that time was running out.

The number of abandoned and rotting boats increased as we moved along. Dilapidated docks, hulls, and pilings insinuated themselves into the landscape as naturally as the scrub pines. The rust and decay that overwhelmed the vessels gave them an awkward charm, a perverse beauty.

Equally intriguing were rusty, working shrimp boats, juxtaposed with pristine, white sailboats, docked side by side, pointing up the diversity of interests on the water. Just over the border between North Carolina and South Carolina after a sharp bend, a beached shrimp boat sat rotting, half on the beach and half in the water. A waterline marked the pitched deck. Everything below the line disintegrated further with each passing wake and tide.

We docked at Barefoot Marina, Myrtle Beach. Across the drawbridge, we wandered in and out of the village of shops and found insulated drinking glasses in a sports store. We bought two of them, Mets for me and Yankees for Tim. We tried to enjoy ourselves, but we knew time was running out.

"What do you want to do?" Tim asked.

"I want to be home by my birthday."

"Yeah, I need to make some calls," Tim said, knowing my birthday was less than two weeks away.

Even with good weather, we still had a long way to go. After five weeks on the water, reality governed our path. The time had come to execute plan B. In the morning, Tim made some phone calls, first to Mike, his helpful guide. Mike recommended a marina and told Tim, "If she still marries you after this, you're a lucky man."

Over the next two days, follow-up calls finalized the plan. The transport company had worked with a marina in St. Petersburg, Florida, in the past. We would go as far as Savannah, where the boat would be hauled out of the water and trucked to Florida. From Savannah, it was a six-hour drive to get home. Six hours. The sound of that, six hours and we'd be home, made the decision easy, but mixed feelings about abandoning our plans lingered. We didn't have any choice, given the time constraints. Way back in Rhode Island, I had had my doubts about the whole adventure, but we had pressed on. The sense of relief I felt every time we safely docked grew tenfold when the ending of our trip became imminent. Like selling the gallery, this journey wasn't a failure. Failure is to never have tried at all.

The weather showed us some mercy, finally, but it was too little, too late. After the four hundred mile ICW marker, we pulled into Georgetown Landing Marina. A sign on the dock warned of alligators, telling me home wasn't far away. Just three more stops, and our grand adventure would enter the next phase, our wedding. It, too, was fast approaching.

We looked forward to our next stop, Charleston. After five and a half hours on the ICW, we passed Sullivan Island. The island was made famous by Stede Bonnet, the "Gentleman Pirate." He had hid on Sullivan Island after escaping from a Charleston prison. Some locals liked the pirates and helped Bonnet break out. The aristocrats saw the pirates as criminals.

Bonnet came from a wealthy family in Barbados. It's not clear why he became a pirate. Marital troubles or boredom may have driven him to take off for Nassau, where he met Blackbeard. Unlike other pirates who captured their ships, Bonnet purchased his. He had limited success as a pirate and was recaptured on Sullivan Island and hanged in Charleston.

The narrow confines of the channel opened in front of us like a door into another world. One minute, marshes and waterfowl surrounded us, and the next, we passed massive barges headed out to sea. Charleston is a peninsula, with the Ashley River to the south and the Cooper River to the north. Fortunately, Charleston City Marina, close to downtown, had space for the night. That evening, we took the marina's shuttle bus into town for a lovely dinner.

"You know, Thanksgiving's around the corner. It's early this year," I said.

"Yeah, Thanksgiving. I don't know how much luck we'll have finding an open marina. I'll ask if we can stay here another night."

In the morning, Tim talked to the dock manager. Yes, we could stay, but we'd need to move to another spot. A large boat had reserved the outer dock where we were tied up. The dockhand gave Tim directions and went to meet us at the slip in the last row up the river.

As Tim pulled away from the dock, the bow pushed through the current. As we rounded the outer dock, the incoming tide broadsided *Little Prince*. The cramped passageway provided little room to maneuver. Tim accelerated to gain control over the powerful rush of water. The balance of enough speed to counter the force of the river, but slow enough to safely turn into the slip, became a battle. Unfamiliar with the particulars of the Ashley River, twice Tim approached the slip but had to back up and try again. Coaxing *Little Prince* into any slip demanded Tim's full attention, but the surging river increased the danger. As we approached a third time, Tim eased up on the throttle before turning the wheel to enter the slip. Without sufficient speed and resistance, the current gained the upper hand. The Ashley River won the battle and slammed us into the docked boats.

A small crowd gathered on the dock, and one by one they realized what had happened. They were familiar with the force of the current and knew docking under those conditions was impossible. Waiting for the tide to turn became our only option. We placed fenders everywhere we could to prevent any further damage. The current held us captive.

CHAPTER 36

THANKSGIVING

Twenty years from now,
you will be more disappointed by the things you didn't do
than those you did. So throw off the bowlines. Sail away from safe harbor.
Catch the wind in your sails. Explore. Dream. Discover.
—Mark Twain

Three hundred years ago, Blackbeard commanded four ships. They formed a blockade of Charleston Harbor and captured several prominent citizens. He demanded mercury, the treatment for venereal disease, in exchange for the prisoners. The pirate's shore leave in Nassau, home to Blackbeard's seventeenth wife, had necessitated the treatment. The pirates threatened to sink all the ships in the harbor and kill the hostages if they didn't get what they wanted. Governor Johnson paid the ransom. The pirates set the hostages free and left for North Carolina.

Our collision reinforced the decision to abandon the trip. For two hours we, too, were held hostage in Charleston, but by a surging tide. Until the tide released us, we remained pinned against the other boats. *Little Prince* sustained a few scratches. The other boats were fine. The marina notified the other boat owners, and Tim called our insurance company.

Docked and ready to move forward with our day, we prepared for Thanksgiving. Dinner consisted of sliced deli turkey, powdered microwavable mashed potatoes, canned green beans, cranberry sauce, a jar of gravy, and a sweet potato pie. Despite all the troubles during our journey, we had a great deal to be thankful for. The trip hadn't gone as planned, but we were fine, healthy, happy, and together. Both of us were willing to take chances, try new things, travel, and let our lives unfold in whatever direction fate dictated. Our Thanksgiving ended with a glorious sunset of pinks and oranges splashed across the sky, silhouetting the sailboat masts and the Robert C. Scarborough Bridge.

The rush and tumult of the previous six weeks slowed to an easy-going cruise. We left Charleston and stopped in Beaufort, South Carolina. Before dinner, we went for a horse-and-buggy tour of the town's historic residences. Mist created a gauzy veil, as though we were looking back in time at the stately homes. Porches adorned with columns and cornices wrapped around both the first and second floors. Some houses had staircases on either side of the entrances, so ladies wouldn't reveal their ankles when climbing the front stairs. That would have been a shameful exhibition.

In the morning, we shoved off, heading for Savannah and the final leg of our nautical journey. The arrangements were already settled at the next marina. No one would be there when we arrived because it was Thanksgiving weekend, but they knew we were coming. On Sunday we toured Savannah before packing up what we would take home with us in a rental car.

Monday morning, November 25, the marina crew in Savannah went to work lowering the flybridge for towing. I stood in the parking lot, legs wobbly from being on the water for so long, and watched as the crew secured lines to pull *Little Prince* around the dock to the waiting lift. The relief in knowing I would be home by evening clashed with the sight of the straps sliding under the dark blue hull of what had been our home for the last six weeks. Sometimes I wanted nothing more than to be home, but returning to "the real world" felt anticlimactic.

Our journey created a unique bond between Tim and me. Six weeks of memories, each day an adventure and an experience like no other. As though a lifetime were compacted into those weeks, we walked away with a feeling of accomplishment. Some people only dream of grand adventures, but we made one happen.

Tim arrived in the rental car. We loaded Tigger and our knapsacks into the back. As we drove through Savannah, Spanish moss hung from live oak trees like tinsel on a Christmas tree. It felt funny to be in a car after weeks on the water. It was also a relief. At home in Gulfport, we had dinner at O'Maddy's Bar and Grille on Boca Ciega Bay and watched the sunset.

The following day, we drove to St. Petersburg to retrieve *Little Prince*. The marina's manager greeted us. I mentioned "our little boat trip."

"That was no little trip," he responded.

Our journey impressed this man who worked at a marina. I had no more regrets.

The art show went up on Friday, with the opening on Saturday evening, and came down at the end of the month. Final preparations for our wedding continued. Six weeks later, the house buzzed with guests and excitement in celebration of our wedding.

"Look," my cousin Juli said as she showed me her wrist. "It's Aunt Mary's charm bracelet." She rolled it around, showing each of the charms. "Here's the typewriter."

We all loved that one because Aunt Mary had started out as a secretary.

"Can I borrow it?"

Juli's smile, with her dimples and big brown eyes, caught my intent. My dress and sapphire engagement ring, in the old setting, covered the old, new, and blue parts. I didn't even think about the "something borrowed" tradition until Juli showed me the bracelet. The delight of following the wedding tradition, with Aunt Mary's familiar charms, filled my heart as Juli put it around my wrist.

Surrounded by family and our closest friends, we gathered at Pass-a-Grille Beach. A warm breeze caressed the blue and white chiffon adorning the gazebo that had been set up for the wedding. My son Mike walked me down the sandy aisle. Tim stood waiting, dressed in a white shirt and blue blazer. His smile, the music, and seeing so many faces of people I loved made my world complete.

As the sun set behind us and the waves rolled into shore, we held hands, said, "I do," and kissed.

In the summer, we returned to Maine to sell the cottage. It was a tough decision for Tim, but necessary. The traveling back and forth, coupled with the expenses of taxes and upkeep, had become too much. He hired a firm to auction the house. We spent the summer packing, selling, and donating the contents. After weeks of sorting through generations of books, furniture, knickknacks, and kitchen gadgets, I needed a break.

"There's an art show this weekend in Peterborough I want to go to. A bunch of people I know will be there," I told Tim.

"I've got a lot to do before the auction. Did you want me to come with you?"

"No, that's fine, I'll go by myself."

The long drive to New Hampshire served as the tonic I needed. As long as we visited Maine in the summer, Peterborough remained within reach. The drive started south on Interstate 95. I continued to Route 101 West. After I passed Manchester, more trees, fewer cars, and familiar sites refreshed my fading memories.

I wondered if this would be the last time I traveled that road. The open windows allowed the scent of pine trees to purge the car of stale air. Tears welled at the thought of abandoning my late husband and son. I accelerated to the top of Temple Mountain and looked across the valley to Mount Monadnock. Whatever changes took place, Monadnock remained the same. I'd painted it so many times I knew the contours of the peak, the way lovers know the curves they caress.

First, I stopped at Agway Lawn and Garden Center. I drove past the barn doors where, years ago, I'd pull up to have fifty-pound bags of horse feed loaded into the back of my red pickup. The garden center, my destination, occupied the opposite side of the building. Nancy, an old friend, was working at the cash register. I picked out plants for Rick and Richard's graves. Nancy and I exchanged pleasantries until she asked what had happened to Richard. Her son, Matt, had been in the same class. As the words fell from my mouth, tears slid down my cheeks. We cried together. I invited her to come to Florida for a visit, though I knew it would never happen.

I left for the cemetery to say goodbye one more time. Each return to Rick and Richard's graves brought to the fore the distance of time. A song could still make me cry, but I no longer allowed myself to sob. On birthdays, anniversaries, and holidays, I glanced back in time, but I didn't linger. Part of me would forever remain with them, in the granitedrunk soil of New Hampshire. Death does not eradicate what was, only what will be. The contrast between my two lives dissolved. It had simply become my life.

I forced my trowel into the earth in front of the granite bench etched with "Busenbark" and dug two holes for the newly purchased plants. I emptied a jug of water onto them and hoped for rain to help them grow so no one would know I had abandoned my husband and son.

Finally, the art show awaited. I parked close to town, got a map showing the location of the participants, and began my visits. Pop-up tents lined the riverbank and walkway throughout the park. Surprised looks and hugs greeted me at every turn. Friendly faces lifted my heart from the sadness that plagued me whenever I looked back. The bitter-sweet reunions awakened the memories of the life I had left behind. I didn't regret leaving, but I missed the feeling of connectedness and belonging.

A drive by my old house completed the trip. The sight of chickens pecking at the ground in front of the house replaced my memories. My little farm, with two dogs, a cat, pygmy goats, a horse, and gardens saturated with flowers, no longer existed.

The pieces of my life fit together. The days of floundering and uncertainty were over. Liberated by the trip to Peterborough, my perspective evolved. It freed me to see the past like a leather-bound collection of photographs, preserved with great care and protected in a safe place like a fine keepsake. The two-hour drive passed easily. I pulled into our driveway in Maine, took in a deep breath of the salty air rolling off Casco Bay, returned Tigger's enthusiastic greeting, and kissed my husband.

The weekend before the auction, we had a party for more goodbyes. We planned to return but as guests, not neighbors. Auction day arrived with realtors, neighbors, and curious cousins standing in the yard. The realtors held their phones up so clients on the other end could hear the auctioneer. Numbers and phrases rolled out over the crowd, repeating bids and chanting familiar lines like "Do I hear . . ." and "We have a bid of . . ." until it ended with "Going once, going twice . . . sold!"

The movers arrived a week after Tim accepted the last bid. He and I were now permanent residents of Florida. Our home in Gulfport worked as a winter escape, but we needed a forever home. During our winters in Florida, we regularly went to open houses to see what other kinds of homes were available. With the cottage sold, we looked at houses more seriously and found one in Bradenton. It had a double front door, of which the realtor had cleverly left both sides open. Inside, light flooded the living room from the grand sliders leading to a pool. We instantly fell in love with the house. It checked off all the boxes of features we wanted.

Two weeks after we moved in, the pandemic descended. We stayed close to home, and I began to write. At first, it centered on the boat trip from Maine to Georgia, but that wasn't the complete story. The more I dove in, the more story there was to tell. The pain and heartbreak of death had become the transition to my new life.

❊ ❊ ❊

When it was safe to travel, we returned to New England. We flew into Boston. During the intervening years since we had sought shelter in Plymouth Harbor, the fully restored *Mayflower II* returned home. After researching Tim's genealogy and information about the journey of the *Mayflower*, I needed to see the restored *Mayflower II*. Knowing for sure that William Brewster from the *Mayflower* was Tim's ninth great-grandfather made returning to Plymouth our pilgrimage. The small size of the ship astonished us.

We continued up to Maine as visitors. We ate lobster and spent time on Bailey Island and in Boothbay Harbor. At the end of our vacation, Tim's cousin Judith brought the family together at her house, across the street from where Tim's cottage once stood. A new house, still under construction, had replaced the cottage.

Casco Bay sparkled beneath the setting sun.

Casco Bay

ACKNOWLEDGEMENTS

When I started to write this book, I thought it was going to be solely about our boat trip. I turned myself into knots trying not to mention the death of my first husband, Rick. The problem of explaining how Tim had years of boating experience and I had none, coupled with our ages, became facts that kept needing explanation. I thought I had completed most of the book when Tim said I should include the events that led me to him. Tim was right.

The cathartic experience of delving into that traumatic time gave me a more thorough understanding of the rhythms of my life. I am grateful to Tim for making that suggestion. It freed me to write what I needed to say. Reliving Rick's death and our life together in such detail evoked a great deal of sadness, but in the end, it completed the story.

I also need to thank my family, in particular my son Mike and my brothers Joe, Bob, and Jim along with their wives, Mary Anne, Barbara, and Debbie. They, and a multitude of friends, are the glue that held me together.

Finally, I need to express my gratitude to the Manatee Writers Group, specifically, William Clapper, Dennis Dunigan, Bart Huitema, Michele Knudesen, Dave Pearce, and Ralf Thompson. They pushed me to be better with constructive suggestions and thoughtful feedback. Thank you, Sue Brite, Bob DeMaura, Peg Gabriel, and Karen Kaiser for being Beta readers. Your input helped clear up some rough edges.

BIBLIOGRAPHY

Apuzzo, Robert, and Michael Cohn. *The Endless Search for the HMS Hussar: New York's Legendary Treasure Shipwreck*. R & L Publishing, 2008.

"Boothbay Harbor Region Chamber of Commerce - Home." Boothbay Harbor Region, 1 July 2022, https://www.boothbayharbor.com/.

Bradford, Ernle. *Drake: England's Greatest Seafarer*. Open Road Media, 2014.

Cawthorne, Nigel. *A History of Pirates: Blood and Thunder on the High Seas*. Chartwell Books, Inc., 2006.

The Conquest of Hell Gate - United States Army. https://www.nan.usace.army.mil/Portals/37/docs/history/hellgate.pdf.

Downey, Christopher Byrd. *Charleston and the Golden Age of Piracy*. The History Press, 2013.

Fortson, Ben. *A Nutshell History of North Carolina*. The History Press, 2016.

"History of Salem, MA: Salem Historical Timeline." Destination Salem, 30 Aug. 2021, https://www.salem.org/salem-history/.

"The History of the Boothbay Harbor Region." Boothbay Harbor Region, 8 June 2021, https://www.boothbayharbor.com /boothbay-harbor-region/history-boothbay-harbor-region/.

"Maritime Museum in Mystic, CT." Mystic Seaport Museum, 30 June 2022, https://mysticseaport.org/.

Museum, Mystic Seaport Museum By Mystic Seaport. *"Mayflower II Restoration Archives."* Mystic Seaport Museum, https://www.mysticseaport.org/category/mayflower-ii-restoration/.

"New Castle NH Historical Society and Old Library Musem." New Castle Historical Society, https://www.newcastlenhhistoricalsociety.org /history--legends.html.

O'Connell, Elizabeth, and Stephen Harding. *Eagle Island: Admiral Peary's Harpswell Home*. Arcadia Publishing, 2017.

Paine, Lincoln P. *Down East: An Illustrated History of Maritime Maine*. Tilbury House Publishers, 2018.

Philbrick, Nathaniel. *In the Heart of the Sea: The True Story of the Whaleship Essex*. Puffin Books, 2015.

Philbrick, Nathaniel. *Mayflower*. Penguin Group, 2006.

Pritchard, R. E. *Captain John Smith, Adventurer: Piracy, Pocahontas and Jamestown.* PEN & SWORD HISTORY, 2021.

"Sailing through Time - Restoration." Sailing Through Time - Restoration, https://sites.google.com/plimoth.org/mayflower-ii -exhibition/restoration?authuser=0.

Sargent, Ruth Sexton. *The Casco Bay Islands.* Arcadia Publications, 1995.

Warner, Charles Dudley. *Captain John Smith.* OUTLOOK Verlag, 2018.

www.ingramcontent.com/pod-product-compliance
Lightning Source LLC
Chambersburg PA
CBHW020444130626
46549CB00001B/292